THE
BYRD MACHINE
IN VIRGINIA

THE
BYRD MACHINE IN VIRGINIA

THE RISE AND FALL OF A CONSERVATIVE
POLITICAL ORGANIZATION

MICHAEL LEE POPE

THE
History
PRESS

Published by The History Press
Charleston, SC
www.historypress.com

Copyright © 2022 by Michael Lee Pope
All rights reserved

Opposite: Author Michael Lee Pope.

First published 2022

Manufactured in the United States

ISBN 9781467139205

Library of Congress Control Number: 2022939458

CONTENTS

Contents

ACKNOWLEDGEMENTS

- To the archivists and librarians in Special Collections at the Library of Virginia who helped me track down old photographs for this book from the Visual Studies Collection.
- To the archivists and librarians in the Manuscripts Room at the Library of Virginia who helped me rummage through dusty executive papers in the State Records Collection.
- To the archivists and librarians at Local History/Special Collections at the Barrett Branch Library in Alexandria who have provided invaluable advice and support.
- And to Hope Nelson, my partner in crime and my inspiration.

WELCOME TO THE MACHINE

The ghost of Harry Byrd continues to haunt Virginia politics. In fact, the influence of the political machine he ran for more than half a century has such a death grip on the public imagination that some people assume it's still humming along, directing events from the great beyond. In reality, though, the machine fell apart decades ago.

But start asking questions about why so few politicians are elected statewide or why governors wield so much power, and you'll soon be haunted by a ghost—a phantom menace constructed decades ago by people long ago might actually shape our shared narrative in ways that might not be immediately apparent. That racist old political machine that closed public schools rather than integrate them might actually have some kind of zombie purchase over the Old Dominion, stacking the deck in favor of the Executive Mansion and pushing the center of power into the back rooms of the Patrick Henry Building, where the governor's minions labor in obscurity.

In recent years, the image of Harry Byrd has taken a well-deserved hit. The statue of him that greeted lawmakers was removed from Capitol Square in 2021, and schools across Virginia are being stripped of his name. The reason for that reevaluation is part of a broader reckoning with the past. If the white supremacy celebrated by a statue of Robert E. Lee was unacceptable on Monument Avenue, then the racist political machine celebrated by the statue of Harry Byrd in Capitol Square must go. And so it was carted away and tucked in some warehouse somewhere to collect dust until someone finds an appropriate way to provide context for it.

When most people think of political machines, cartoon images of Tammany Hall or Boss Tweed immediately come to mind. Certainly, the corruption of urban politics in the Gilded Age still holds a rarified space in the American mind. But political machines in the South worked very differently. The "good old boy" networks of small-town Dixie used a combination of patronage and electioneering to maintain power, although usually on a much smaller scale than James Pendergast in Kansas City or James Michael Curley in Boston.

Here is where the Byrd Machine defied the odds. It was bigger and more powerful and more enduring than the big-city bossism that took root in metropolitan America. Even among southern political machines, there was something about the lasting statewide significance of the Byrd machine that eclipsed Boss Crump in Tennessee or even "Kingfish" Huey Long in Louisiana. From his perch as longtime chairman of the Senate Finance Committee, Byrd controlled Virginia politics with a kind of animal instinct that identified the instruments of control and then prevented anyone else from coming close.

"The Byrd Machine is an oligarchy, composed of the few, chosen by the few to make decisions for the many," noted *TIME* magazine in 1958. "In its oligarchic context, the Byrd organization is an alliance of gentlemen, and a gentleman is known more for his philosophy than by his purse or pedigree."

The birth of the Byrd Machine is often traced to the day Harry Byrd became chairman of the Democratic Party of Virginia in 1922, a position he used to carefully oversee the flow of money and power. At the time, he was a young state senator from the Shenandoah Valley who had been born with a silver spoon in his mouth—someone with a colonial pedigree and a father who would soon become Speaker of the House of Delegates.

The Byrd Machine was a statewide operation, but it operated as a network of courthouse rings. Sheriffs, judges and clerks of court conspired to hold power by using the mechanics of elections to control outcomes. For these Democratic Party officials, the bad old days of widespread voter participation led to anarchy and violence. They believed that the best way to uphold the principle of democracy was to limit who got to participate. The poll tax was the weapon of choice to control who was allowed to vote and, therefore, who was allowed to win.

Opposite: Harry Flood Byrd Sr. ran a political machine for half a century of Virginia politics. *Library of Congress.*

Above: The Byrd family had its roots in colonial America, a blueblood tradition that gave him and his children a head start in life and in politics. *Library of Virginia.*

"It's like a club, except it has no bylaws, constitution or dues," explained Lindsay Almond, one of the Byrd Machine governors. "It's a loosely knit association, you might say, between men who are the philosophy of Senator Byrd."[1]

Byrd's last name gave him a sense of nobility and prestige. But that wasn't the only thing he inherited. The political machine he ran was constructed from the remains of the Martin Machine, a political organization from a previous era when railroad money was used to grease the wheels of power. Interestingly, the Martin Machine was a reactionary move intended to vanquish the Mahone Machine, a raucous coalition of Black Republicans, estranged Democrats and poor farmers. So, Byrd may have inherited a machine that had deep roots in Virginia politics, but he perfected its operations and carefully guarded the front door. It was "one of the most durable and powerful political organizations in the country," explained *New York Times* Virginia correspondent Cabell Phillips in 1949.

"It has become as much a fixture in the comfortable, cloistered life of the people of the state as, say, their faith in the Confederacy or their addiction to buttermilk biscuits and Smithfield ham," Phillips explained. "To relate Senator Byrd to this palpable monolith is a little like debating the divine origin of the Scriptures. You know the answer, but try to prove it."[2]

At the age of twenty-one, Harry Byrd served an appointed term on the Winchester City Council. He lost reelection to the position, the only time he was ever defeated at the polls. *Library of Virginia.*

Byrd's last name gave him a sense of nobility and prestige. But that wasn't the only thing he inherited. The political machine he ran was cobbled together from the remains of a previous machine. *Library of Congress.*

The center of power for the machine was the county courthouse, where organization functionaries kept the engine humming along. In election after election, county seats across Southside Virginia and up and down the Shenandoah Valley to the Eastern Shore competed with one another to see who could provide the most lopsided victory to machine candidates. The old Confederate statue guarding the courthouse was a not-so-subtle hint that retrograde forces were at work. Few people held as much power or had as much influence as the local clerk of court, who was welcomed in the back room of the senator's Washington office and the hotel suites of his lieutenants in Richmond.

"There will always be a certain mystique surrounding the manner in which the organization picked its candidates for governor," explained historian Harvie Wilkinson. "From the informal give and take of courthouse preferences, the Senator's own wishes, and the choice of the Senator's closest advisors, a preferred candidate usually emerged and proceeded to an almost certain victory in the forthcoming Democratic primary and general election."[3]

Courthouse clerks organized local elections for the organization candidate, aided by the sheriff and the commonwealth's attorney. Members of the local board of supervisors worked as the public face of the campaign team, as did the delegation to the General Assembly. Behind the scenes, the chief judge of the circuit court would encourage support for the organization candidate by offering to use his power to appoint key positions in the jurisdiction. The bread and butter of any political machine is patronage, and in the Byrd Machine, it flowed through the courthouse during election season as judges named members of everything from electoral board and the school board to the welfare board and the board of reassessors.

"Candidate appearances also featured a handshaking tour near the courthouse, followed by impassioned eloquence before a small but sympathetic courtroom crowd," explained Wilkinson. "Large fans hanging from the high ceilings to break the heat of a July afternoon, light-green courtroom walls broken only by faded pictures of county fathers and former circuit judges, Harry Byrd grimly warning of a grasping federal

Harry Byrd had a pathological hatred of debt. *Library of Virginia.*

government—such was a classic snapshot which would soon take its place beside the New England town meeting and presidential whistle stop in the gallery of fond political memories."[4]

Critics of the machine accused it of offering inferior services, pointing to meager appropriations for education, health and welfare. They denounced a structure designed to suppress opposition, lamenting a poll tax used to suppress the vote and a patronage ring operating out of the local circuit court. They pointed out the bloated salaries of machine officials, whose paychecks were calculated by a three-member State Compensation Board appointed by the governor. They criticized the refusal of Virginia Democrats to support the national party, which started moving in a different direction during the New Deal and never looked back. Some of them even pointed out the oppressive and virulent attitude toward Black Virginians, a mainstay of the organization that would eventually be its downfall.

But the machine endured, steamrolling opposition thanks to a political system of domination it inherited from a previous generation. At the center of the Byrd Machine's reason for existence was a conservative belief in parsimony, perhaps even a pathological hatred of debt. This was rooted in Harry Byrd's personal history as well as lingering resentments from the Civil War. These Virginia Democrats maintained what they called a "golden silence" when it came to big-spending national Democrats. In some ways, silence became an organizing principle for the organization.

"The senator himself smilingly denies that he takes more than a remote, avuncular interest in the internal affairs of the state," explained Phillips.[5]

The heyday of the Byrd Machine would also become its mayday, massive resistance. That's when the crusty old worthies decided that the public schools would be better off dead than miscegenated. From Front Royal to Charlottesville and Norfolk, classrooms were shuttered, and children suffered the consequences. Even today, children of the era speak of how they lost an important part of their childhood because chieftains of the Byrd Machine couldn't see fit to follow the demands of *Brown v. Board*.

Ultimately, of course, they lost the legal fight. And the political fight. And the culture war. And they were shown the exit as the Democratic Party imploded as segregationists became Republicans and massive resisters became a joke. It would take several decades for the Harry Byrd's reputation to fall into such ill repute that his statue was carted away by state workers and secreted into the realm of obscurity. Gone but certainly not forgotten.

These days, the Byrd Machine is a distant memory. But it's one that's worth detailing because of the grip it continues to hold on the folkways of power even today. The machine may be gone, but its ghost continues to haunt Capitol Square.

Chapter 1

THE MAHONE MACHINE

How a Confederate General Became the Leader of a Progressive Interracial Political Machine

The Byrd Machine was not the first political machine in Virginia. It was also not the second. Like any respectable drama, the tale of Virginia political machines unfolds in three acts—a story of clashing ideology and statecraft that shares a singular organizing principle: power.

The first political machine was constructed by William Mahone, a former Confederate general who led a progressive organization that included Black voters and Black elected officials. The second political machine was organized by Thomas Staples Martin, a railroad tycoon who worked with conservative Democrats to crush the progressive movement and implement Jim Crow racism in Virginia. All of that paved the way for Harry Byrd, who inherited the remains of the Martin Machine and reworked it to suit his own purposes.

Harry Byrd often gets credit for running Virginia's most successful political machine, and he certainly ran the most powerful and durable machine in Virginia political history. But the inventor of machine politics in Virginia is a distinction that rightfully goes to William Mahone, a former Confederate general whose meteoric rise to power was matched only by his breakneck fall from grace. Mahone was so exacting with his wardrobe that his tailor said he would rather make dresses for eight women than one suit for the senator. He spoke with a squeaky voice and stood at five-foot-six, weighing in at about one hundred pounds soaking wet. But don't let that fool you. He ran a cutthroat operation that seized power after Reconstruction and kept its steely grip on Virginia politics as long as possible.

"In the whole gallery of Southern figures of his generation, he stands out as one of the boldest and most enigmatical," wrote historian C. Vann Woodward. "Mahone was a self-made man, not to the manner born, yet possessed of an imperviousness of will and manner and an overweening confidence in his destiny."[6]

Mahone is a man of contradictions: hero of the Lost Cause who created America's most successful biracial coalition; railroad tycoon who became the hero of the working man; and enemy of the establishment who became a political boss. His machine ended the poll tax, abolished the whipping post, boosted funding for asylums, forced the railroads to bear a larger share of the tax burden and repudiated a third of Virginia's debt. It increased the appropriation for public education by 50 percent and opened scores

HON WILLIAM MAHONE
UNITED STATES SENATOR
VIRGINIA.

William Mahone was "a self-made man, not to the manner born," wrote historian C. Vann Woodward, "yet possessed of an imperviousness of will and manner and an overweening confidence in his destiny." *Library of Virginia.*

of new schools across Virginia. It was also a ruthless and autocratic organization that relied on forced campaign contributions from government employees who wanted to keep their jobs and businessmen who wanted state contracts.

"The legislation was mostly economic and social, intended to subserve the interests of the masses and to break the power of the privileged classes," wrote historian Charles Chilton Pearson. "As the machine became perfected, it shaped both appointments and legislation more and more to suit its own ends until it became a very real and a very debasing tyranny."[7]

A native of the tiny unincorporated community of Monroe in Amherst County, Mahone was raised in a world of pitched racial politics and escalating sectional animosities. When Nat Turner led a bloody slave revolt that killed more than fifty people in an insurrection, Mahone's father was part of the militia that hunted him down. Young Billy Mahone developed a reputation as "a devil on wheels," according to one Boston newspaper.

"He smoked, chewed, cussed like a pirate and gambled like a Mississippi planter," the *Boston Traveler* wrote of young Billy Mahone. "He was the leader in all deviltry, and the terror of all good country mothers whose boys occasionally went to town. Every good boy was cautioned to look out for that 'bad little wretch, Billy Mahone.'"[8]

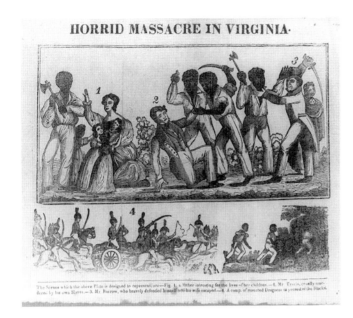

HORRID MASSACRE IN VIRGINIA·

When Nat Turner led a bloody slave revolt that killed more than fifty people in an insurrection, William Mahone's father was part of the militia that hunted him down. *Library of Congress.*

He spent some time at the Virginia Military Institute but decided that this was not the life for him. Instead, he launched himself headlong into the world of railroading. Mahone worked for several institutions in rapid succession: the Orange and Alexandria Railroad, the Fredericksburg and Valley Plank Road Company and the Norfolk and Petersburg Railroad. By the time he turned twenty-seven, he was chief engineer of the Norfolk and Petersburg Railroad. By the time he was thirty-three, he was president.

It was during this time in his life that he married Otelia Butler of Smithfield in Isle of Wight County, who apparently wielded a significant amount of influence on her husband and left a lasting impact on Virginia geography. Because she was a fan of historical Scottish fiction and the medieval adventure novel *Ivanhoe*, several place names along the Norfolk to Petersburg line bear names that reflect her taste in literature: Wakefield, Windsor, Waverly and Ivor. At the end of the line, an infamous argument between the Mahones led to a curious name.

"When the train stopped a few miles short of Petersburg, the local of the final depot, the Mahones got into a tiff," explains the *Virginian Pilot.* "They apparently could not agree on a name. Hence Otelia made up Disputanta, and it stuck."[9]

By the time the Civil War erupted in 1861, Mahone was a slave owner and a secessionist. Because of his military training, he was appointed lieutenant colonel of the Sixth Volunteer Virginia Infantry. He was quickly promoted

The Waverly train station is one stop on the Ivanhoe tour of medieval names inspired by Otelia Butler Mahone, wife of the Readjuster's political boss. Other stops on the whistle tour include Wakefield, Ivor and Windsor. *Library of Virginia.*

to colonel and then brigadier general and ultimately general. He fought at Seven Pines, Manassas, Fredericksburg, Chancellorsville, Gettysburg and Spotsylvania Courthouse. His counterattack at the Battle of the Crater earned him the nickname "Hero of the Crater."

After the war, Mahone threw himself back into to the railroad business with a renewed sense of purpose. He returned to his work at the Norfolk and Petersburg Railroad and also became president of the South Side Railroad, with a goal of eventually merging them into the Virginia and Tennessee Railroad. Unfortunately for Mahone, this plan ran afoul of the traditional powerbrokers in Richmond. But he was able to persuade lawmakers to consolidate his railroads into the Atlantic, Mississippi and Ohio. For Mahone, it was a first taste of politics. And it was thrilling.

In 1877, Mahone threw his hat into the ring for governor. But it was not to be, at least not yet. That was the year Frederick Holliday of Winchester was elected governor as a Conservative Democrat. Mahone initially supported the Conservative Democrats, but he soured on their stubborn insistence on paying down the state's debts. The issue of Virginia's debt would eventually become central in Virginia politics, a fulcrum that helped propel Mahone to power and then eventually pull the rug from under him.

After the war, Virginia faced a debt of $45 million. Most of that was prewar spending on things like railroads and canals, about $33 million.

Much of that was spent in the western part of Virginia, which became West Virginia during the war. Many in Virginia questioned why they should have to pay a debt on improvements to another state. By the time Reconstruction in Virginia ended in 1870, the debate over the debt had become the most significant issue in Virginia politics.

Mahone sensed an opportunity. So, he founded the Readjuster Party, a group whose central organizing principle would be readjusting the debt rather than paying it in full. Conservative Democrats, sometimes known as Funders, had passed the Funding Act in 1871, requiring Virginia to pay two-thirds of the debt and handing the remainder of the bill to West Virginia. The move left little room for financing almost anything else, especially public education.

By 1879, opposition to the Funding Act had grown to a fever pitch. Mahone leaned into the controversy and covered a convention in Richmond in late February of that year. The newly formed Readjuster Party included rural whites from the Shenandoah Valley and Blacks from all over the commonwealth, who played no part in contracting the debt and certainly didn't benefit from it.

Mahone was not the only big personality in the party. The Readjusters also included John Massey, who called himself the "father of the Readjuster movement," a mesmerizing stump speaker who could spellbind rural audiences. It also included former Delegate Harrison Holt Riddleberger, editor of a newspaper known as the *Tenth Legion Banner*. During his time in the House of Delegates, Riddleberger initially sided with the Funders but later concluded that the privileged classes had their thumb on the scale and switched sides.

The Readjusters also had their own newspaper, the *Richmond Whig*. Edited by William Elam, the newspaper served as a clearinghouse for answering all the assaults made in the other papers. Elam accused wartime Governor William "Extra Billy" Smith of stealing from the Confederate treasury. The governor's son, Colonel Thomas Smith, resented the implication and demanded an apology. The two men ended up meeting for a duel at the Oakwood Cemetery in Richmond. Elam had the first shot but missed. Smith's bullet struck Elam's chin, smashing his jawbone and knocking out four of his teeth.

"Carried to the house of a friend, Elam survived the episode—though severely weakened," wrote historian James Moore. "Colonel Smith, on the other hand, gave every appearance of enjoying the whole affair. Indeed, he subsequently presented the two dueling pistols to William L. Royall, the vitriolic Funder newsman, as mementos."[10]

The Funders expected to prevail against this ragtag group of upstarts. But the Readjusters were on to something. They tapped into a hatred of the ridiculous sense of honor Conservative Democrats had about the debt. And their promise to keep schools open, pay teachers, abolish the whipping post and invest in insane asylums resonated with an electorate that was sick and tired of austerity. The Readjusters won forty-five of the one hundred seats in the House of Delegates and twenty-four of the forty seats in the state Senate.

The newly elected General Assembly met in December and promptly elected Mahone to the U.S. Senate. Riddleberger, who was now a state senator, introduced a bill to scale down the debt. The bill swiftly passed through the House and the Senate, but Governor Frederick Holliday vetoed it. Holliday's veto message explained that public schools were a luxury, not a necessity.

"This veto will carry our party on a tide of prosperity for two years, and we shall sweep the state—making Re-adjustment a fixed achievement against all combinations, all machinations, all the powers that can be mustered against us," responded Riddleberger on the floor of the state Senate. "We are for the people, and the people are for us and with us!"[11]

The Readjusters realized that they would need to install one of their own in the Executive Mansion if they intended to accomplish their goal. In 1881, they nominated lawyer and newspaper editor William Cameron of Petersburg as their candidate for governor. The Funders selected State Senator John Daniel of Lynchburg as their candidate. The Readjusters scored a clean sweep, installing Cameron in the Executive Mansion and giving Readjusters large majorities in the House and Senate.

Members of the General Assembly selected *Shenandoah Herald* publisher Harrison Riddleberger as the other U.S. senator, joining Mahone in Washington. Their timing couldn't have been better. In September 1881, Chester Arthur became president following the assassination of James Garfield. Arthur threw his support behind the Readjusters, allowing Mahone to use federal patronage to his advantage. In return, Mahone became a Republican, which allowed the party to take control of a closely divided Senate.

"Mahone was the undisputed boss of this widely ramified machine," wrote historian Virginius Dabney. "He was anxious to build a machine that would maintain a steely grip on the state for an indefinite period."[12]

Now that they held all the levers of power, Readjusters in the General Assembly passed a bill readjusting the state debt. It was similar to the one former Governor Holliday vetoed. But now Cameron was in the Executive Mansion, and he signed it. The new bonds, known as "Riddlebergers,"

Left: Newspaper editor William Cameron become governor in 1882, when the Readjusters controlled large majorities in the House and Senate. *Library of Virginia.*

Right: Newspaper editor Harrison Riddleberger served time in the House of Delegates and state Senate before becoming a United States senator. He was so creative with financing Civil War debt that 3 percent bonds became known as "Riddlebergers." *Library of Virginia.*

This 1881 engraving shows the excitement behind the Readjuster Party, which sought to readjust the Civil War debt to ease the burden on war-torn Virginia. *Library of Virginia.*

would be issued bearing 3 percent interest. The remaining debt would be assumed by West Virginia.

"No greater boon can be given this people than a speedy, equitable, and final settlement of all controversy concerning State debt," Cameron said in his first message to the General Assembly.[13]

Dispatching the debt question was only the beginning for the Mahone Machine. Cameron and the Readjusters then set about to make investments in public education and higher education, including schools for Black students with Black teachers. Lawmakers also appropriated $100,000 for the Normal and Collegiate Institute for Negroes in Petersburg and the Central Hospital for mentally afflicted African Americans, also in Petersburg.

The whipping post was abolished. The poll tax was eliminated. Taxes on corporations were increased, especially the railroad robber barons. Taxes on real estate were reduced. Funding was increased for the Virginia Agricultural and Mechanical College at Blacksburg, later known as Virginia Tech.

But the era of Mahone wasn't just about progressive politics. It was also a time for revenge. The machine-controlled legislature fired all the justices of the Virginia Supreme Court, as well as three quarters of the circuit court judges and corporation court judges. Funders weren't just turned out at courthouses. They were also removed from boards of educational and charitable institutions.

Mahone's ruthless tactics were anything but subtle. He demanded officeholders contribute a fixed percentage of their salaries to the Readjuster war chest, 5 percent for state employees and 2 percent for federal employees. Businessmen who scored state contracts were expected to share the wealth and help finance party activities. Readjusters who held office were required to sign pledges agreeing to support bills and candidates approved by the caucus. Mahone built a political machine unlike anything Virginia had ever seen, and its willingness to work with Black citizens to form a government created racial resentments that would last well into the next century.

"When he sought to build up a political machine which would be under his complete personal domination, some of his ablest leaders, as well as the people, began to revolt," wrote historian Allen Moger in the 1940s. "Mahone's prostitution of office and officeholders, his corrupt manipulation of the Negro vote, and his dictatorial management of his party were anathematized by the term Mahoneism, which came to include everything disreputable in Virginia politics."[14]

It's true that Mahone benefited from the support of Black voters. But was that the spoils of corrupt manipulation? That view overlooks the benefits he delivered for his voters. He expanded educational opportunities for Black Virginians, although they were segregated schools. His work to abolish the racist specter of the whipping post as a form of public punishment was a lasting reform to the criminal justice system. His investments in asylums and social services undoubtedly benefited Black people.

And Mahone used his power and influence to distribute patronage. Norfolk had a Black postmaster. Black men were appointed doorkeepers in the House of Delegates and state Senate. They received clerkships in state offices and became guards at the state penitentiary. Black teachers were given jobs at Black schools.

Does all that add up to "corrupt manipulation," as Moger argued in 1942? On one hand, Mahone was running a political machine that demanded money from state workers and contractors, which he used to finance his party operations and distribute patronage. On the other hand, he used the power of his machine to help the Black voters who put him in office. Whether any of that amounts to corruption or manipulation is probably a matter of interpretation.

Mahonism took its most extreme form in Danville, which is where the seeds of its destruction were sown. Under a charter granted by the Readjuster legislature, Black voters elected a majority of Black members to the town council of Danville in 1882. Nearly half of the police officers were Black men, and all the justices of the peace were Black magistrates. White businessmen responded by publishing a document known as the Danville Circular in October 1883, attacking Readjuster rule in general and African Americans in particular.

"Negro women have been known to force ladies from the pavement and remind them that they will learn to step aside next time," the businessmen wrote. "It is a very common practice for the negroes who are employed about our homes to allude to white ladies and gentlemen as men and women and to negroes as ladies and gentlemen....They do it to irritate and throw contempt upon the white race."[15]

The businessmen expressed outrage about corrupt courts, gerrymandered districts and a lopsided tax burden. They complained about "the scene of filth" at the market stalls occupied by Black vendors and "crowds of loitering and idle negroes, drunkenness, obscene language, and petit thieves." The timing of the Danville Circular was significant because it came just before a General Assembly election, electrifying an already tense situation with racial animus.

"Can anything be imagined better calculated to bring on a row?" asked the *Staunton Spectator*.[16]

An 1883 race riot in Danville became an unlikely turning point in Virginia history, ending the Mahone Machine and opening the door to an era on conservative rule. *Library of Virginia.*

Racial tensions erupted into a conflagration the Saturday before the election of 1883 in what became known as the "Danville riot," an unlikely turning point in Virginia history that ended the Mahone Machine and opened the door to an era on conservative rule. It all began when a white man struck a Black man shortly around lunchtime. The white man was Charles Noel, a clerk in his twenties, as he was walking by two Black men at the H.D. Guerrant & Company store on Main Street. He later testified that one of the two men "came near knocking my left foot from under me."

"I was getting out of the way of a lady, and a white lady at that," the man explained, according to testimony from Noel.[17]

The idea that the Black man might have accidentally tripped a white man in an effort to avoid causing a problem for a white woman was apparently good enough for Noel, who said he continued on for about three paces when one of the Black men commented to the other Black man that it didn't make a "damned bit of difference whether it was all right or not; he can't do anything about it." Noel thought that was "insolent," so he responded by punching one of the Black men. They responded by punching him back. The fight spilled off the sidewalk and into the gutter.

Within minutes, a crowd assembled there on Main Street. Noel said that two Black men in the crowd began to draw pistols. Noel left the scene and went home to have lunch. He later returned to town and dropped by the Opera House, where Democrats were holding a political meeting in advance of the election. When Noel explained what had happened in the altercation, the mob of angry whites flooded out into the streets and confronted the crowd of Black men. Shots were fired. Pandemonium erupted. Chaos ensued.

When the smoke cleared, four men lay dead in the street—one white man and three Black men. In the days that followed, another Black man died from his wounds received that day, and the white community organized a militia and began armed patrols. Democrats seized on the race riot and weaponized the issue against the Readjusters. The City of Danville launched an official investigation into the violence, creating a Committee of Forty that heard from thirty-seven witnesses. Ultimately, the committee concluded, the problem was that Danville's African Americans had become "rude, insolent and intolerant to the white citizens of the town."[18]

The story of the Danville riot spread far and wide, by word of mouth on horseback and by telegraph. The *Chicago Tribune*, a Republican newspaper, called it the "Danville massacre." The *New York Times* headline shared this view of events, as indicated by the headline in the Gray Old Lady: "Inoffensive Negroes Shot Down in Great Numbers of Inflamed Whites." The view of what happened on November 3, 1883, and who was to blame was a Rorschach test for views about race and politics.

The political fallout from the Danville riot was swift, and it demolished the Mahone Machine. The Democratic Party won back control of the General Assembly, and the Readjusters would soon become a distant memory. Within a few years, Mahone and Riddleberger would be out of the Senate. These days, the memory of the political and social clout won by African Americans during this era seems counterintuitive—a lost chapter of history that forms a counterpoint to everything we think we know about how white supremacy gripped Virginia's politics after the Civil War.

State and federal employees in Virginia were no longer required to fork over a fixed percentage of their salaries to the Readjuster Party. Businessmen who scored contracts were no longer expected to share the wealth with the Mahone Machine, and the political patronage dried up. In many ways, what came next was a reaction to the Mahone Machine—a new system of conducting elections to make sure Black people would be shut out of power for generations to come.

Chapter 2

THE MARTIN MACHINE

Railroad Magnate Seizes Control of a Party and a Commonwealth

The dramatic rise and fall of William Mahone left an important mark on Virginia politics, a machine that reached from the U.S. Senate through the governor's office into appointments to boards and commissions. During its brief but dramatic season in power, the Mahone Machine created an infrastructure of a political machine that was remarkably far-reaching, extending to the election machinery of judges and registrars and clerks of court.

After the Danville riot helped unseat the Readjusters in the House and Senate, the first order of business for the new Democratic majority in the General Assembly was to break the grip of the Mahone Machine. Since Mahone's hand-picked governor was still in the Executive Mansion, his power of appointment was revoked. Boards and commissions were stripped of their powers, and new members were appointed. Congressional districts were redrawn. Town charters were rewritten to require new registration of voters.

Then the investigations started. Lawmakers launched inquiries into Mahone's lieutenants, revealing fraud, corruption and violent partisanship. The point was reclaiming power

HON. JOHN S. BARBOUR.

"We hold the fort," declared Democratic Party chairman John Barbour. "And we have come to stay." *Library of Virginia.*

rather than punishing wrongdoing, and a key part of the strategy for the Democrats was adopting the raison d'être of the Readjusters. With the issue of readjusting the debt out of the conversation, the Democrats were able to regain their foothold.

"We hold the fort," declared Democratic Party chairman John Barbour. "And we have come to stay."[19]

Tall and spare with white hair and a bushy mustache, Barbour was the organizational genius behind the redemption of the Democratic Party. The son of a congressman, Barbour was a longtime president of the Orange and Alexandria Railroad who followed in his father's footsteps and got himself elected to a seat in Congress. He used the tools of the Mahone Machine, creating a new political machine to demolish the old political machine. For Barbour, the key to seizing the reins of power was making sure Democrats controlled elections

Thomas Staples Martin used a "yellow dog fund" from railroad lobbyists to purchase a U.S. Senate seat. He would later boast it was "an earnest effort to keep the Democratic party in power and maintain Anglo-Saxon supremacy." *Library of Virginia.*

and installing party loyalists as the custodians of ballots and judges of elections. This was accomplished by passing the Anderson-McCormick election law, which authorized the General Assembly to appoint members of electoral boards.

"The law made possible a system of election control and election frauds," explained historian Allen Moger.[20]

Now that Democrats had a majority in the General Assembly, they were able to finally control the election machinery the way Mahone had done so skillfully and so ruthlessly. The law was clearly aimed at demolishing what was left of the Readjuster coalition, seizing power in Richmond by stuffing the ballot box in every city and county across Virginia. It opened the floodgates to bribery and fraud, making intimidation and corruption the coin of the realm. Democrats would literally stuff the ballot box with multiple votes printed on tissue paper, depositing several votes at once. Judges would often find more votes than voters in a system that was ruthlessly efficient but also tenuous.

The nephew of Robert E. Lee, Fitzhugh Lee was elected governor in 1885. Thomas Martin's victory over Fitzhugh Lee for a U.S. Senate seat in 1893 was one of the greatest upsets in Virginia political history. *Virginia Historical Society.*

"Its hold was precarious because it rested on a foundation of manipulation of the suffrage and assertions that all whites should vote Democratic," wrote historian Richard Hamm. "Any issue that divided the white Democratic vote could bring about a Democratic disaster."[21]

Barbour's protégé was a lawyer from Scottsville, Thomas Staples Martin, who was counsel for the Chesapeake and Ohio Railroad. After the war, the Chesapeake and Ohio Railroad purchased the Orange and Alexandria Railroad. The merger brought Barbour and Martin together in a business relationship, although it was politics where the pair formed a political machine that would keep the trains running on time for decades to come.

A year after the Anderson-McCormick Act gave Democrats in the General Assembly power to control every electoral board in Virginia, Martin secured a spot on the Democratic state central committee. Then he went about installing his people in office. Former Confederate General Fitzhugh Lee was elected governor in 1885. Congressman John Daniel replaced William Mahone in the Senate in 1887. And Barbour himself replaced Harrison Riddleberger in the other Senate seat in 1889.

When Senator Eppa Hunton announced that he would not seek another term, the railroads created a "yellow dog fund" to direct campaign cash toward Democrats who pledged their support for legislation that would be beneficial to the railroads. Martin used the slush fund to purchase himself a seat in the U.S. Senate, one of the most brazen acts of ring politics in Virginia history. When members of the Democratic legislative caucus were choosing a candidate, they overlooked former Governor Fitzhugh Lee in favor of Thomas Staples Martin on the fourth ballot. The vote was sixty-six to fifty-five.

"It takes money to run the machine," explained former Governor Andrew Jackson Montague. "While politicians of Virginia calmly deny that there is a machine in this state, it is known in every state in the union that no state has a machine so heartless and so grinding as that in Virginia."[22]

Martin's victory over Lee in 1893 was one of the greatest upsets in Virginia history and perhaps also one of its most corrupt moments. It prompted an immediate investigation, although no evidence emerged to prove a quid pro quo. Years later, when a series of letters was unearthed in 1911 exposing how railroad money was used to install Martin in the U.S. Senate, the machine boss defended his actions as "an earnest effort to keep the Democratic party in power and maintain Anglo-Saxon supremacy." Essentially, the excuse for corruption was racism. Delivering a speech in Leesburg, he explained that the letters revealed "my work for the maintenance of Democracy and white supremacy."

Congressman Claude Swanson agreed with William Jennings Bryan that "you shall not crucify mankind upon a cross of gold." His free-silver politics caught the attention of the Martin Machine. *Library of Congress.*

"What is there in these letters to impeach me?" asked Martin. "They were written during a crisis in the Democratic party. In 40 counties, the negroes had a majority, and some of them were school trustees. I worked on several executive committees to get money to secure the rule of the white man and the permanence of Anglo-Saxon civilization."[23]

When Martin arrived in Washington, D.C., he set about to build a political machine that would last many years into the future. He was joined in this effort by Congressman Claude Swanson and Delegate Henry "Hal" Flood. Swanson would later use his position in the machine to become governor and ultimately secretary of the U.S. Navy. Flood (who was the uncle of Harry Byrd) would go on to serve in the state Senate and ultimately twenty years in the House of Representatives.

"Being a man of quiet ways and unostentatious manner, he did not for a time attract much attention," explained the *Richmond Times-Dispatch*. "People spoke of him as a business senator."[24]

The source of their power was railroad money. They used it to control the General Assembly through a network of supporters in courthouses across the commonwealth. In the early years, the Martin Machine struggled to build a durable organization in an era of fierce political battles over free silver and prohibition of alcohol. In 1901, Martin supported Congressman Claude Swanson for governor. But Martin and his favored candidate had a strong challenge from progressive Attorney General Andrew Jackson Montague, who campaigned against the influence of the Martin and his machine.

"He is more autocratic than Mahone was," Montague said in one debate. "For the latter broke down the door and let people know he was coming. Senator Martin believed in secret methods and did not come out and fight his battles in the open."[25]

Martin was dealt a blow when Montague won the election, and he set his sights on building an organization that could forge compromises between warring factions of the Democratic Party while simultaneously attacking Republicans as the party of Reconstruction and Readjusters. At the same time, increasing frustration with elections created a movement to dump the old Underwood Constitution from 1870 that allowed so much participation from Black voters. Montague was a strong

Top: Henry "Hal" Flood was the uncle of Harry Byrd. He was a longtime congressman from Shenandoah Valley, and he was chairman of the Committee on Foreign Affairs when the United States entered World War I. *Library of Congress.*

Bottom: The election of Andrew Montague Jackson as governor in 1901 dealt a blow to the Martin Machine, which was supporting Claude Swanson as the organization candidate. *Library of Congress.*

Carter Glass got his start as editor of the *Lynchburg News*. He played a major role in creating Jim Crow restrictions in the constitutional convention that created the 1901 Constitution. As a U.S. senator, he helped craft the Glass-Steagall bill, which separated commercial banking from investment banking. *Library of Congress.*

advocate for writing a new constitution, which was viewed as a progressive reform to protect elections from corruption.

"Vote buying, ballot-box stuffing and assorted varieties of political thievery were notoriously widespread," wrote historian Virginius Dabney. "A principal argument for a convention was that elections in Virginia had become so shot through with fraud that something had to be done."[26]

Between 1874 and 1900, no fewer than twenty Congressional elections were officially contested. Allegations of election fraud in Norfolk almost caused a gun battle in the General Assembly in March 1900. Growing concern about the dangers of too much democratic participation caused a forty-two-year-old newspaper editor turned state senator to enter the picture and advocate for a constitution specifically designed to disenfranchise Black voters. State Senator Carter Glass, editor of the *Lynchburg News*, helped steer the 1902 constitutional convention toward a poll tax and a new era of Jim Crow white supremacy.

The Martin Machine quietly opposed the idea of a constitutional convention, although it could see that momentum was building. When Democrats gathered for their state convention at Norfolk in 1900, the Martin Machine tried to work against a resolution endorsing a convention. But they found themselves in the minority. The progressives were clearly gaining ground. A statewide referendum asking voters if they wanted a constitutional convention passed with a comfortable margin, and Senator Glass was able to move forward with his plan to disenfranchise whites and Blacks alike.

"Our politics will be purified, and the public service strengthened," declared Glass at the constitutional convention on April 4, 1902. "This plan of popular suffrage will eliminate the darkey as a political factor in this State in less than five years so that in no single county in the commonwealth will there be the least concern felt for the complete supremacy of the white race in the affairs of government. And next to this achievement in the vital consequence will be the inability of unworthy men of our own race, under altered conditions to cheat their way into prominence."[27]

Clearly, this was an era before white supremacists realized that they needed to couch their rhetoric in language that at least tried to obscure their racism. These days, the idea that progressives would want to disenfranchise Black voters seems counterintuitive. But in the early 1900s, the movement to limit the franchise was viewed as a good government initiative to remove corruption from politics.

Just as the progressives were putting together their new constitution, they were also electing a governor, Andrew Jackson Montague, who was attorney general at the time. In the election of 1901, he beat out the Martin Machine candidate, Congressman Claude Swanson. On the campaign trail, Montague supported party primaries, better schools, improved roads and responsibility of employers for injured employees. Montague's victory in the 1901 Democratic primary was a blow to the Martin Machine, and progressives undoubtedly assumed that their new constitution would help them maintain power.

"Republican government founded upon an electorate without intelligence is a house whose foundations is sand," Montague said in his inaugural address. "The age of the hand is past, and the age of the machine has come."[28]

Montague was talking about machines as a tool of industrial progress, although he could have well been talking about the political machine that was about to demolish him and his movement. As it turns out, the new constitution ended up strengthening the machine position of dominance. With the exception of the State Corporation Commission, which regulated the railroad industry at the center of the machine, the constitution ended up giving the machine a gift that kept on giving: a dramatically reduced electorate and a courthouse ring of sycophants who used the levers of power to keep themselves in office.

"The reform of the electorate boomeranged on the reformers," wrote historian Wythe Holt. "It reduced the electorate by one-half, removing that voting power at the bottom which probably would have supported reform."[29]

The test for progressives came in the next election in 1905. Montague hoped to build on his successful administration by taking out Senator Martin, but he came up short. The dramatically reduced electorate caused by the new constitution ended up helping the machine and harming progressives. Martin beat Montague, and voters also installed machine lieutenant Congressman Claude Swanson in the Executive Mansion, which must have been sweet revenge after being denied the seat by the progressives four years earlier.

Richard Evelyn Byrd, the father of Harry Byrd, became Speaker of the House after just two years in office. *Library of Virginia.*

The election of 1905 also brought a new face to Richmond: a young new House member named Richard Evelyn Byrd, the father of Harry Byrd. The primary that year featured a hotly contested race between the senior Byrd and Alvin Tavenner. Byrd won, but Tavenner contested the election. The fight was heated, and each side become embittered toward the other—a hostility that became violent at the Burgess Hotel on North Main Street in Winchester. That's where the junior Byrd confronted Samuel Chiles, the county treasurer and a close personal friend of Tavenner.

"Hot words followed, and a desperate encounter ensued," the *Woodstock Shenandoah Herald* reported. "Both exchanged blows in rapid succession, until the proprietor, S.D. McDonald, and others separated the combatants."[30]

The campaign between Byrd and Tavenner was apparently heated and bitter, and it was a fight in a political sense as well as an interpersonal one. When Byrd won the election, Tavenner and his supporters claimed voter fraud. They contested eleven out of nineteen precincts, creating an intense showdown between the rival campaigns. The local Democratic Party initially refused to release the election returns but then relented and shared the numbers. The rising suspense was apparently too much for the young Byrd, who instigated the brawl.

"Both bear marks of the fight," the newspaper reported. "The affair caused a tremendous sensation and is the leading topic of conversation."[31]

The progressive era in Virginia politics was shockingly brief. After Montague's four years in power, the conservative political machine returned to power with the election of Swanson. Having survived an existential challenge from the progressives, the Martin Machine was now controlled by a group that came to be known as the Big Four: U.S. Senator Thomas Staples Martin, Governor Claude Swanson, Congressman Hal Flood and Richard Evelyn Byrd, the father of Harry Byrd, who became Speaker of the House after just two years in office.

"Mr. Byrd is a man of popularity, both at home and in the Legislature," noted the *Richmond Times Dispatch* when he became chairman of the influential Courts of Justice as an incoming freshman. "He is recognized as one of the strongest lawyers in the upper valley section of Virginia."[32]

As Montague's term in the Executive Mansion was drawing to a close, he set his sights on dislodging Martin from his Senate seat. It was a replay of the 1901 campaign, although the rules of engagement had changed dramatically. The number of progressive voters had been extremely curtailed by the new constitution. And this time voters would decide the Senate candidate rather than the General Assembly.

"For the first time in the history of Virginia, the people of the State will vote for a United States Senator next Tuesday and it will be up to them to say on that day, whether or not they appreciate this privilege or prefer a senator selected by machine methods, without regard to their wishes in the matter," observed the *Accomac Peninsula Enterprise*, which said that Martin's first election revealed his corrupt nature. "It will also be remembered that the charge was then made and not since disproved that his election was due in some way to machine methods, or in other words, that he was backed by the railroads," the newspaper explained. "That machine methods controlled and gave him a second term as United States Senator too is charged and many voters in the State, a majority of them, perhaps, believe justly."[33]

As Election Day approached for the Democratic primary in 1905, tempers flared in the sweltering August humidity. It was a campaign featuring heated rhetoric and fiery speeches. The *Richmond Times-Dispatch* noted at least one fight on Main Street, "where one man knocked another down twice for making sweeping denunciation of the friends of the other candidate and applying an offensive epithet." In another instance, a Martin supporter and a Montague supporter almost came to blows after insults and disparagements were exchanged.

"Oh, don't get mad about it," one of them said as the incident blew over.[34]

Montague and the progressives came up short. Martin was reelected to a third term in the U.S. Senate, and Claude Swanson was elected governor. The machine was now humming with perfect political precision. Martin became minority leader in the Senate, and Congressman C.C. Carlin began pushing for Martin to get the nomination for president. Fellow Virginian Woodrow Wilson ended up snagging that nomination and winning the election, but Martin was still gaining power. He became chairman of the Appropriations Committee and ultimately majority leader in 1917.

"Mr. Martin's experience as a legislator has been extensive, and his knowledge of governmental affairs is equaled by few public men," editorialized the *Washington Post*. "His tact in dealing with his colleagues, his personal popularity, his fairness in all things, his long service and his ability to devise acceptable plans for majority action—all qualify him admirably for the position of majority leader."[35]

During World War I, Martin oversaw the greatest expenditure of revenue ever made by the government of the United States at that time. The strain of that responsibility took a toll, and Martin's health may have been one of the casualties of the war. When Republicans seized control of the Senate in March 1919, Martin became minority leader. Eight months later, he died in Charlottesville, and the future of the machine was in doubt.

"For more than twenty years, this Virginian was a master of the party politics of his state," wrote the Washington journalist Jesse Frederick Essary. "He himself never suffered defeat as a candidate. And few of the men whom he nominated for office and behind whom he threw his full strength were rejected at the polls."[36]

The enduring legacy of Thomas Staples Martin was the machine that bore his name, at least for a time. The Martin Machine would fix the rules of the game to ensure an outcome in favor of the conservative political organization. Never again would the Readjusters be able to conspire with Republicans to seize the reins of power. By the time Martin was buried at the University of Virginia Cemetery in 1919, he had developed the party into a force of nature that had enough power to create its own weather.

With Martin gone, though, Virginia now had a machine without a leader. The void would not last long.

Chapter 3

OUT OF THE MUD

Senator Byrd Takes the Road Less Traveled to the Executive Mansion

T he seeds of the Byrd Machine were sown in a muddy clump of earth on the road to the inauguration of Elbert Lee Trinkle. It was a bitterly cold February morning in 1922, and the governor-elect was driving his Lincoln through Orange on his way to Richmond. A layer of wet snow had transformed the road into an unworkable mess, and his automobile became mired to the axle. It was that moment—a frustrating experience with a substandard highway at the very moment the young state senator was poised to seize power—that may have changed his life forever. It would set in motion a series of events that would have Trickle slogging through a number of embarrassing policy shifts and ultimately the rise to power of State Senator Harry Byrd.

By the 1920s, the rise of the automobile was putting new pressure on an old problem: the deplorable state of Virginia's highways. Before the Civil War, Virginia borrowed heavily to build roads and turnpikes. After the war, that debt was paid at face value, and roadbuilding became a county problem. But the rise of the automobile created new political momentum, and Governor Claude Swanson created a new state highway department in 1906 to administer matching funds to local governments.

Some localities made more progress than others. Winchester and the Shenandoah Valley had excellent roads. Other parts of the commonwealth slogged along in the ruts. The governments with good roads employed a mix of state funds, convict labor and county debt. Some scheduled "road days," when volunteer laborers and horses would contribute to infrastructure as a

Left: Elbert Lee Trinkle was a lawyer from Wytheville who became party chairman in Wythe County and served in the Senate before being elected governor. His support for debt-financing highway construction was weaponized by his enemies, who had a pathological hatred of borrowing money. *Library of Virginia.*

Right: George Preston Coleman was a controversial state highway commissioner, deciding where roads should be located, what materials should be used and even the order of construction. *Library of Virginia.*

community good. Other local governments faced opposition, like the owners of a towing business that blew up a stretch of road near Dumfries to benefit themselves financially.

Borrowing money was at the center of the financial strategy. In 1920, voters overwhelmingly approved a constitutional amendment to allow for a system of serial bonds to finance highway construction. It wasn't even close. The margin of victory was more than two to one. But that doesn't mean that the idea of borrowing money to build roads didn't have growing opposition. Farmers were concerned that the attention would go to modern highways for tourists rather than roads they could use for agriculture. Shenandoah Valley politicos suspected that they would be forced to fork over money for roads in other parts of Virginia.

Some of the opposition was personal, and it was directed at one man: George Preston Coleman. The controversial state highway commissioner operated with few checks and balances, deciding where roads should be located, what materials should be used and even the order of construction. He was imperious and autocratic, raised in a house that his ancestor St. George Tucker purchased from Edmund Randolph in 1788.

"He had much of the fine sense of noblesse oblige that had been handed down to him from his illustrious Tucker ancestors," explained the *Richmond Times Dispatch*. "A gentleman in all of his instincts and in his dealings with his fellow-man, he held high the torch handed down to him from the past."[37]

A native of Williamsburg, Coleman was educated at the College of William and Mary and then served as an engineer in Mississippi, Georgia, West Virginia and Minnesota before returning to Virginia to take a position as assistant highway commissioner in 1906. In 1911, Governor William Hodges Mann appointed him the highway commissioner, and Coleman set out on a plan to favor a primary road system at the expense of a secondary road system. His minions stopped and weighed trucks to make sure that they were using the right kind of tires.

Perhaps most detrimental to his political future, he loved borrowing money. Speaking to various associations around Virginia, he implored people to press lawmakers to build roads as fast as humanly possible—even if that meant going into debt to make it happen. That caused suspicion in rural Virginia, which feared that secondary roads would be sacrificed on the altar of tourism. By the end of 1921, Coleman had become so toxic that his absence at a conference of road experts "occasioned some comment," noted the *Accomack Peninsula Enterprise*.

"Although Mr. Coleman was in the city," the newspaper reported, "it developed he was not invited to the conference."[38]

He wasn't invited to the party because his public image was a cookie full of arsenic, the sweet smell of unchecked power mixed with the poisonous disregard for rural areas financed by unholy debt. This was a time of shifting politics in Virginia, and Coleman was part of the scene that was fading away. Thomas Staples Martin died in 1919, leaving the political organization without a leader. Then, in 1921, chairman of the state Democratic committee Rorer James died. That same year, Congressman Henry "Hal" Flood of Appomattox died. All these deaths left a political void, and several groups were eager to step in and seize power. The Martin Machine was fading away, and a new generation was seizing the reins of power.

The 1921 Democratic primary provided the perfect opportunity for transition. The previous election saw the Democrats on their heels, losing the Executive Mansion to independent Democrat Westmoreland Davis in a three-way race with independent John Garland Pollard and the Martin

Machine candidate, Democratic Lieutenant Governor James Taylor Ellyson. Davis appointed longtime machine adversary Carter Glass to the U.S. Senate and encouraged organization antagonist Henry St. George Tucker of Rockbridge to run for governor. For several months, Tucker had the race all to himself. But the Democratic Party was not about to let him run away with its machine.

Enter forty-four-year-old Elbert Lee Trinkle, a large and vigorous lawyer from Wytheville who became party chairman in Wythe County and was eventually elected to the state Senate in 1915. Now in his second term, he tried to stake out a position for himself as the progressive candidate in the primary. Trinkle supported suffrage for women and prohibition against alcohol. Tucker, on the other hand, was viewed by some as the anti-machine candidate. He opposed prohibition and women's suffrage. Both candidates initially opposed a bond issue to finance highway construction, although Trinkle had a bad habit of flip-flopping on the issue. Politicians across Virginia aligned to the machine withdrew their endorsements for Tucker and threw their support behind Trinkle.

By May, Trinkle was ready to lay out a more comprehensive position on highway construction. At the center of his platform was a proposal to reorganize the highway department. Borrowing money, he said, was out of the question. He dubbed the proposal "Forward, Not Backward," pledging a "business administration by a businessman." In the end, he said, lawmakers would make the call and a final resolution would be made by voters.

"It would not be wise for me to recommend to the new General Assembly that any bill should be passed committing Virginia to a bond issue of $50 million or any fixed amount," Trinkle announced.[39]

Trinkle was trying to have it both ways. The carefully worded statement gave the impression to voters that he was against a bond issue. But Trinkle limited his comments to the "next General Assembly," leaving open the possibility that things might change after the next election. It might have been a mixed message, but a young senator by the name of Harry Byrd liked what he was hearing. He had twenty thousand copies of Trinkle's statement printed at his own expense and distributed throughout the Shenandoah Valley.

Trinkle ended up with twenty-three thousand more votes than Tucker in the August primary. The general election victory against Republican Henry Anderson was more lopsided, a historic sixty-thousand-vote margin of victory. No governor had ever arrived at the Executive Mansion with such a decisive mandate.

The inaugural ceremonies were ominously scuttled because of unusually cold temperatures. Instead of a large outdoor ceremony on the steps of the Capitol, festivities happened inside the House of Delegates. Trinkle's inaugural address outlined a complete reorganization of the State Highway Department, creating a new five-member commission that would have the power to appoint an engineer. The new governor framed the idea as a progressive approach to contemporary government.

"The times in which we now live demand that Virginia have a modern highway system, and we must fully recognize that the day of the impassable and badly constructed roads should no longer be tolerated," Trinkle declared in his inaugural address. "The quickness of our state growth along all lines is to bet greatly measured by the speed which we develop in our highway construction work."[40]

Financing the new highway program would be accomplished by a new one-cent gas tax. Significantly, though, Trinkle did not rule out borrowing money to finance highway construction—essentially leaving that decision up to lawmakers if they wanted quick action. He certainly didn't discourage the idea.

"We must recognize this great truth that it costs money to build roads, and that the speed with which they may be built is entirely dependent upon the amount furnished for this purpose," he said. "And you, gentlemen of the General Assembly, have upon you the solemn duty of deciding this question."[41]

By the time the General Assembly gaveled back into session, Senator Byrd was ready with legislation to reorganize the highway department. It replaced the current commission and commissioner with a ten-member commission—one for each congressional district. Byrd had another trick up his sleeve, an investigation into the highway department. The resolution launching the investigation would discredit Coleman, build support for the reorganization and allow Byrd to attack his enemy on the public stage.

Senators were also considering a separate proposal, one introduced by Senator C. O'Connor Goolrick of Fredericksburg. Goolrick disagreed with Byrd about bonds, and his bill was designed to placate Coleman's enemies by reducing the powers of the commissioner. Over in the House, Delegate Thomas Ozlin of Lunenburg County introduced a compromise measure known as the Byrd-Ozlin bill. Coleman would stay on as the highway engineer, a move designed to win over his friends and take advantage of his years of experience. Instead of a ten-member commission, the Byrd-Ozlin bill created a five-member highway commission whose members would be

GEN. C. O'CONOR GOOLRICK

SEN. HARRY FLOOD BYRD

Above, left: Senator C. O'Connor Goolrick of Fredericksburg offered a compromise designed to placate George Coleman's enemies by reducing the powers of the commissioner. *Library of Virginia.*

Above, right: State Senator Harry Byrd launched an investigation into the highway department, discrediting George Coleman and setting the stage for a run for governor. *Library of Virginia.*

Right: Delegate Thomas Ozlin of Lunenburg County introduced a compromise known as the Byrd-Ozlin bill. It created a five-member highway commission whose members would be appointed by the governor. *Library of Virginia.*

THOMAS W. OZLIN

appointed by the governor. Trinkle signed the bill, although he privately expressed concern that the debate killed any room to borrow money.

"Opponents of Mr. Coleman are so mad there is very little hope to handle them in any way that is effective," Trinkle wrote to an associate. "Propaganda such as this kills the bird that laid the golden egg, and it looks like road development will be delayed another two years."[42]

Trinkle decided that he needed to do something dramatic. So he made an appearance at the Norfolk Committee of the Woodrow Wilson Foundation and made a shocking declaration: He had actually been *for* bonds all along, and he was simply waiting for the right moment to reveal his true intentions. He told the crowd that cheap labor and low interest rates made a bond issue irresistible, especially if the highway department was reorganized. Senator C.C. Vaughn of Franklin, who was also president of the Good Roads Association, introduced a bill that would allow for a $12 million bond program. Trinkle tried to gaslight lawmakers.

"In the campaign, I, at no time, expressed any views as to a road bond issue," said Trinkle, adding that he wanted to correct "some rather inconsiderate and inaccurate statements."[43]

Trinkle had clearly changed his position, but now he was trying to make it sound like he was in favor of borrowing money all along. The lie upset lawmakers who were adamantly opposed to borrowing money. But supporters believed that the bait-and-switch was working. Trinkle and his supporters believed that they had pulled one over on voters.

"His attitude on a conservative bond issue for good roads in Virginia will have the approval of every right-thinking citizen in the Old Dominion," observed the *Alexandria Gazette*.[44]

The crowd in Norfolk may have eaten it up, but the knives were already out for the turncoat governor. During a joint session of the General Assembly on March 3, 1922, the governor showed up in person to throw his support behind the Vaughn bill. He told lawmakers that they needed to determine if they wanted good roads or not. And if they did want good roads, they needed to figure out if they wanted them built quickly or slowly.

Critics worried that one bond issue would lead to others and that some areas of the state would benefit at the expense of other parts of the state. The House passed Vaughn's bill with an amendment requiring a referendum in the 1922 general election. Senator Byrd led a parliamentary move to reject the amendment, and the House responded by refusing to appoint a committee to resolve the deadlock. The General Assembly adjourned without taking action.

Goolrick was furious. He told the Associated Press that the House of Delegates was an "ignorant body of leaderless, irresponsible reactionaries who would wreck any construction plan."[45]

Just as soon as the General Assembly session ended in a stalemate, talk of an extra session began. The governor said that he would only call one if people expressed an overwhelming desire for it. Political operatives in the

Fighting Ninth Congressional District were worried that a fight might hurt the party in the 1922 election, and they sent letters of the governor asking him to postpone the session—at least until after they were able to unseat incumbent Republican Congressman Bascom Slemp.

The folks in the Fighting Ninth weren't alone. Democrats were also preparing for a hotly contested primary fight for the U.S. Senate seat held by Claude Swanson against former Governor Westmoreland Davis. The last thing Democrats wanted was to have their incumbent senator ousted in a primary. Nevertheless, Trinkle hit the road and made speeches all over Virginia advocating for a bond issue. He argued that good roads would help bring northern industry to the South and end the days of the one-room schoolhouse.

"Don't blame me for your roads," Trinkle said in Tappahannock. "I have done everything that can be done by me to give Virginia adequate highways."[46]

Eventually, Trinkle gave up on the bond issue. For him, the more important objective was the road program. He didn't particularly care how it was funded. Many lawmakers had been elected on an anti-bond ticket, and the governor came to realize that passing a bond issue would leave many voters feeling betrayed and jeopardize the Democratic Party. So he called for an extra session in late February 1923 to provide emergency funds for highway construction. In the weeks leading up the session, Senator Byrd met with Governor Trinkle and struck a deal: Trinkle would get the bond advocates to stand down in exchange for Byrd securing a gas tax of at least three cents per gallon.

"The people of Virginia can easily provide on the pay-as-you-go plan more than $50 million for new road building within the next six or seven years," Trinkle told lawmakers. "This amount ought to be sufficient to meet the reasonable expectations of a progressive people."[47]

Advocates for borrowing money to finance road construction were still holding out hope, though, because lawmakers ended the special session by creating a referendum on the issue. Voters would ultimately decide the issue at the ballot box that November. The coalition of forces aligned to support the referendum included Coleman, Goolrick, the Virginia Good Roads Association, the Virginia Bankers Association and the *Richmond News Leader*. It was an impressive group, although they were no match for the opposition Byrd was about to create for their referendum.

The campaign featured a bewildering array of arguments for and against the referendum, including enough contradictory figures to leave voters dizzy and confused about which side was right and which side was looking to bamboozle taxpayers. Ultimately, the pay-as-you-go side won in a landslide, thanks in part to opposition organized by Byrd. Using his connections as chairman of the Democratic Party, he created a committee to oppose the referendum in each congressional district. Then he installed trusted local leaders to oversee the effort.

One of Byrd's chief concerns was the current state of the roads. He knew that if the roads were a mess, voters would be more willing to approve the referendum to borrow money to fix them. So he repeatedly pressed the governor to improve the state of the roads before voters went to the polls in November. He also worked with a Louisa candidate to unseat Goolrick in the August primary, an indication of the machine power Byrd was beginning to wield.

"Here was an example of the methods of the new Organization," explained historian Stanley Willis. "Increasingly, there would be less room in it for those who chose to follow paths even slightly inimical to the dominant faction."[48]

Advocates for the referendum were hopeful that foul weather on the eve of the referendum would help their cause. But anti-bond forces flooded the ballot box. Although a few cities approved of the idea of borrowing money to improve roads, voters up and down the Shenandoah Valley rejected the idea. So too did rural farming communities in Southside and central Virginia. Harry Byrd had martialed his forces into a statewide operation, and he had created a name for himself promoting a system of pay-as-you-go government. He also earned a reputation for himself as a political leader who had an iron fist concealed under a velvet glove.

"With the victory, the Byrd era publicly began," concluded Willis.[49]

Chapter 4

THE RISE OF HARRY BYRD

How a Blueblood Scion of a First Family Becomes a Political Boss in the Old Dominion

Harry Byrd was born with a silver spoon in his mouth, although it was a tarnished antique. His family could trace its history back to the bluebloods of the seventeenth century, a time when William Byrd arrived on the banks of the James River and fought in Bacon's Rebellion. His maternal grandmother was a daughter of Charles James Faulkner, a U.S. senator and minister to England. By the time Harry Byrd was born in the summer of 1887, Virginia was a place of genteel poverty.

"Paint was peeling off the noble Corinthian columns of the great mansions; roofs were leaky, or obviously patched," wrote historian and Byrd family chronicler Alden Hatch. "And every man over thirty he knew could remember the Federal troops, the carpetbaggers, and going hungry because of devastated fields, stolen cattle, and the wreckage of the economy."[50]

Byrd did not inherit vast wealth, but he did inherit power. Not only did he have that gold-plated last name, but he was also the son of Richard Evelyn Byrd. Harry Byrd's father, known as Mr. Dick, was a prominent apple grower and newspaper publisher in Winchester who would go on to get himself elected to the House of Delegates and eventually become Speaker of the House. But young Harry didn't approve of the way his old man ran the newspaper into the ground. Advertisers were notoriously late paying for their spot in the paper, and many skipped out altogether. By the time the debt to the Antietam Paper Company had grown beyond $2,500, the company refused to ship any more paper on credit.

This is when a teenage Harry Byrd dropped out of high school and took over the *Winchester Evening Star*. Admittedly, this was kind of nuts. He was barely fifteen years old, but he had already developed a remarkable aptitude for business. Perhaps another factor contributing to this was his elder brother's exploits. Rear Admiral Richard Evelyn Byrd Jr. had just returned from a widely celebrated tour around the world. What could young Harry possibly do to top that? Conjugating verbs at the Shenandoah Academy probably seemed kind of insignificant in comparison. And so the teenager presented his father with a request: let him drop out of school and take over the bankrupt *Evening Star*.

Harry Byrd was born with a silver spoon in his mouth, tracing his history back to the bluebloods of the seventeenth century. *Library of Congress.*

"Everyone in Winchester undoubtedly thought Mr. Dick was crazy," explained Hatch.[51]

It may have been crazy, but it worked. The fifteen-year-old put on his first suit with long trousers and headed across the Potomac River to Maryland, where the Antietam Paper Company was headquartered. He had little leverage to negotiate, and he had no money to offer. But he developed a plan to sell to the paper executives. The idea was that the company would ship one day's supply of paper each day, and the newspaper would pay in cash. Pay as you go.

The folks at Antietam were sold, and they agreed to the arrangement—shipping newsprint in exchange for cash on delivery each day. The next order of business was tracking down all those Winchester businesses that owed money for advertising. If the *Star* went out of businesses, Byrd argued, they would have only one advertising option: the *News Item*. That was the rival newspaper, owned by George Norton, and it would have a monopoly unless all those unpaid bills were handled.

So there he was, scurrying around Winchester to pick up five dollars here, three dollars there, selling an advertisement or two. He would reach the train station just in time to pay cash for newsprint for that's day's edition. His penny-pinching management style worked, and Byrd was eventually able to buy a small inventory of newsprint. The modest stockpile would ensure that the *Winchester Star* would be published even if the railroad to Maryland

Top: Richard Evelyn Byrd, known as Mr. Dick, was a prominent apple grower and newspaper publisher in Winchester who would eventually become Speaker of the House of Delegates. *Library of Virginia.*

Middle: Secretary of the Navy Claude Swanson presents a medal to Rear Admiral Richard Evelyn Byrd in 1937. *Library of Congress.*

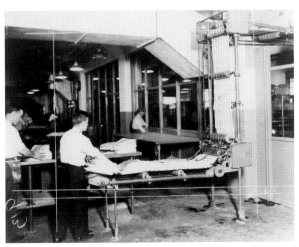

Bottom: When a young Harry Byrd inherited the *Winchester Star*, the paper was in desperate financial shape. So he cut a deal with the Antietam Paper Company to buy one day's supply of paper each day, paying in cash to avoid debt. *Library of Congress.*

The Valley Turnpike, U.S. 11, connects the north and south through the Shenandoah Valley. *Library of Virginia.*

wasn't up and running. Eventually, he insisted on paying off the newspaper's entire debt, $2,500, even though the paper company was willing to forget about it.

Winchester was not big enough for two newspapers. James Thompson was a wealthy publisher best known for his long tenure at the *New Orleans Item*; he lived in Summit Point, just over the West Virginia line. He suggested to Byrd that he buy the *News Item*, which at first seemed like an impossible dream. But it happened. Byrd ended up purchasing the paper at Thompson's suggestion for $2,500 and then closing it down.

Having conquered the newspaper industry in Winchester, Byrd started setting his sights beyond his hometown. He took a gig as manager of the Southern Bell Telephone Company, a job that paid sixty dollars per month. Then, in 1908, he talked his way into becoming president of the Valley Turnpike Company. That's the group that owned the Valley Pike, the only paved highway in Virginia. He became president during a moment of transition, and he made it profitable.

"The Valley Pike was rapidly deteriorating due to the advent of motor traffic," the *Richmond Times-Dispatch* noted, adding that Byrd turned the fledgling organization around and eventually turned it over to the state without cost, including toll houses and machinery. "During this period, the Valley Pike was one of the first roads in the country to experiment with the bituminous binder."[52]

For Byrd, it was a piece of family history—it was the same road William Byrd used to fight in the French and Indian War. It was also the road General Philip Sheridan used during the Valley Campaigns of 1864. By 1908, it was a macadamized stretch of road connecting Winchester to Staunton with toll booths every few miles. A trip between the two cities cost $4.75, which would be well over $100 in today's dollars.

The newspaper business and the plum spot on the turnpike company were not the keys to Byrd's financial fortunes. The secret to his success was being part of the Virginia apple industry. As a nineteen-year-old, he made the owner of an apple orchard just beyond the railroad tracks in Winchester an offer he couldn't refuse. Byrd struck a deal that he would purchase his crop and harvest it. For the orchard owner, it was a way to focus time and attention on other matters.

The apple growing business is an exercise in timing. April and May offer a wild card, providing a potential heat wave that could tank the entire crop. A heat wave could force the delicate blossoms too early, allowing a cold snap to shrivel them. On the other hand, a long, cold winter could complicate matters. As a harvest manager, Byrd had to look out for drought, rain and insects.

The deal was a success, and Byrd went on to make similar arrangements at other orchards. He bought a spray rig and recruited a team of workers. The young man in a hurry would make a point of working beside them in the orchard, sometimes working eighteen hours a day spraying and thinning the apples. Considering his family's wealth and status, there was really no need for him to work so hard. But young Harry Byrd was driven.

He continued taking on more and more orchards, eventually assembling a crew of workers. During apple season, they lived in a truck that was like a house on wheels, a vehicle that also carried the spray rig and tools. All that hard work paid off, and by 1911, he was able to save up enough capital to buy a plot of land on Hawthorne Drive in Winchester for an orchard of his own. Byrd and his crew planted the apple trees and then set about the business of nurturing them into production.

The next year, in 1912, he struck up a partnership with Episcopal rector William Smith and bought the Rosemont Orchard, which was about nine miles east of Berryville. This particular orchard was always one of Byrd's favorites because it was on land from Cottage Farm that his ancestor Thomas Taylor Byrd settled in the Shenandoah Valley back in 1786.

Although his formal education was limited, he developed an extensive knowledge in the art and science of apples. These days, visitors to the Shenandoah Valley will find a relatively limited number of varieties growing

Byrd grew sixteen different kind of apples, including Ben Davises, Albermarle Pippins, Grime's Goldens, Staymans, Yorkshires, Winesaps, Wealthies and Smokehouses, to name a few. *Library of Virginia.*

among the orchards of Frederick County. But Byrd grew sixteen different kind of apples, including Ben Davises, Albemarle Pippins, Grime's Goldens, Staymans, Yorkshires, Winesaps, Wealthies and Smokehouses, to name a few.

Some were sweet. Others were tart. Some were early bearing. Others came late. Some were firm. Others were mealy. The modern apple industry has less variety because people tend to like large apples that are red or golden. Byrd's orchards yielded all kinds of shapes and sizes. Many varieties were significantly smaller than a Golden Delicious. Most of Byrd's early crops were shipped over to Europe, where the appearance of the apples is less significant. By the time he was elected governor, Byrd had become one of the most prominent men in the Virginia apple business.

"He is now perhaps the largest individual orchardist east of the Mississippi, giving personal and direct attention to all details of the business," noted the *Richmond Times Dispatch* in 1926. "He has his own selling and manufacturing organization selling in the country, South America, Cuba and Europe."[53]

As he developed his orchards, Byrd became an innovator. He followed changing trends in taste, and he would swap out new varieties for unpopular ones. He experimented with new methods of spraying and labor-saving tools. He worked with other fruit growers in the area to organize Winchester Cold

Storage, the largest storage exclusively for apples in the world. He bought a horse and buggy to keep track of his expanding clutch of orchards. But that wasn't fast enough for the young man in a hurry. So he bought a motorcycle he used to zoom through blossoming apple groves and bump along farm roads full of ruts.

Newspapering and apple growing wasn't enough for young Harry Byrd. He also caught the political bug, and he caught it early. Before he was even old enough to vote, he was working for the local Democratic Party and learning the ropes from Winchester party leaders. At the tender age of twenty-one, he became a member of the Winchester City Council. He was fortunate to have a political mentor in his father, Richard Evelyn Byrd, who was then a member of the House of Delegates working his way toward becoming Speaker of the House. Then there was his uncle, Congressman Henry "Hal" Flood of Appomattox, who was working his way toward becoming chairman of Foreign Affairs Committee.

"During the years when he was getting on his feet financially, Harry Byrd was content to remain a member of the City Council and good party worker, while his relatives became increasingly powerful," noted Byrd biographer Alden Hatch.[54]

During the bizarre election of 1912, a three-way race featuring a former incumbent running as a third party, Byrd's father served as a delegate to the Democratic National Convention. The senior Byrd ended up playing a key role in defying Senator Thomas Staples Martin and swinging part of the delegation to Woodrow Wilson. He and Wilson studied law together at the University of Virginia, and Wilson would later appoint Richard Evelyn Byrd as the U.S. attorney in the Western District of Virginia. Martin supported Alabama Senator Oscar Underwood, who lived in an estate in Northern Virginia often described as the most haunted house in America, Woodlawn Plantation. One of the highlights of the convention was a speech by William Jennings Bryan demanding that Virginia multimillionaire Thomas Ryan be withdrawn from the Virginia delegation.

"The Baltimore convention may yet be remembered largely as the place where Hal Flood, of Virginia, gave William J. Bryan some valuable information on the Democratic doctrine of State's rights," noted the *Richmond Times Dispatch*. "The results showed that Speaker Byrd, the Virginia Wilson manager, was correct in his forecast that he would get at least nine votes in the delegation for his man."[55]

Wilson was elected, and the new president routinely consulted Speaker Byrd about federal appointments in Virginia. That gave the Speaker of the

House of Delegates control over federal patronage, dramatically expanding his influence. A few years into the Wilson administration, in 1914, the president appointed Speaker Byrd as U.S. attorney for the Western District of Virginia. The Speaker resigned from the House of Delegates and opened a new law office in Richmond with his son Tom, who had recently graduated from the University of Virginia.

"No one could trick a hostile witness into damaging admissions more suavely than Mr. Dick, and no one could squeeze tears from a jury's eyes more eloquently," explained Hatch. "He was a superb orator, far better than his son, Harry, even though the latter climbed much higher up the political ladder."[56]

By 1915, young Harry Byrd was ready for his spot in the Virginia Senate. He was only twenty-seven at the time, but he had a successful career in newspapers, apples and Winchester politics. He arrived in Richmond as an energetic lawmaker, snagging a spot on three committees. Not only did he grab a key position on the Finance Committee, but he also served on the Elections Committee and the Roads Committee. It was an era when the machine was humming along silently in the background.

"The Organization was functioning as quietly as a Rolls Royce and there were no controversial local issue," noted Aldon.

Freshman Senator Byrd walked into the Senate chamber as someone who had already made a name for himself leading the Valley Turnpike Company, which put him in a position to discuss roadbuilding as an authority. He objected to a lack of maintenance and excessive administration costs. He suggested that native materials be used instead of imported ones and excoriated the existing state road law as unworkable.

"The law is based upon the false theory that the construction of a costly type of road is permanent and makes no provision for maintenance," Byrd wrote in a statement delivered to newspapers. "That is the theory, but the fact is that these costly so-called permanent roads have rapidly disintegrated."[57]

Byrd's first General Assembly session wasn't just about roads. Lawmakers were also considering a proposal to create a college for women that might complement the all-male University of Virginia. They were reviewing a plan to create a "commissioner of morals" to oversee shipping provisions. The Anti-Saloon League was pressing for the ouster of officials who failed to enforce prohibition laws. Byrd's scheme to radically transform how state funds were used to build roads must have seemed a bit grandiose coming from a freshman senator who was not yet thirty years old.

Freshman senator Harry Byrd (*top row, seventh from the left*) entered a Senate chamber that was bitterly divided over the issue of prohibition. *Library of Virginia.*

"Instead of a well-planned road system, there would be confusion and waste," editorialized the *Richmond Times Dispatch*. "The entire administration would lie in the hands of men whose experience is open to question."[58]

Across the Atlantic, the outbreak of a world war was dominating the headlines. In Virginia, business was booming. Labor and management were both in agreement with the farmer about the value of war orders from England, France and Russia. The flood of prosperity created a strong inclination toward the status quo. Why rock the boat when the *Lusitania* had already sunk? Attention turned to the Allies and whether America should enter the war on their side.

In Richmond, Byrd was making a name for himself as a liberal member of the Senate. Along with Senator Willis Robertson of Martinsburg and Senator O'Connor Goolrick of Fredericksburg, Byrd was part of a bloc in the Senate that supported worker's compensation and school improvements. They also wanted to create new protections for working children. At the foundation of all those arguments was the underlying issue of roads. How could Virginia pull itself out of the mud without a plan?

"The maintenance and construction of roads is essentially local," Byrd argued. "It is local because local labor and local material is required and because familiarity with local conditions is necessary to economical management."[59]

Wilson finally got around to asking Congress for a declaration of war against Germany in 1917, and it was Harry Byrd's uncle Hal Flood who sponsored the bill in the House. Flood was chairman of the House Foreign Affairs Committee, and his support for a declaration of war was part of a patriotic spirit that was spreading like wildfire at the time. Harry Byrd's two brothers joined the military—one was sent to an officer's training camp, and the other became a naval aviator at Pensacola. For the rest of his political career, critics would cast shade at him for ducking the war to handle business, family and politics.

After the war, Byrd became chairman of the Virginia State Democratic Committee, an organization led by party leaders who exercised authoritarian control. His election as chairman was an indication of his status as an up-and-coming force, although the position wasn't as

Bishop James Cannon was a fanatical Methodist prohibitionist, helping to create the Anti-Saloon League in an effort to root out business activities of a group he called "drunkard makers." *Library of Virginia.*

powerful as it may sound. U.S. Senator Claude Swanson was theoretically in control of the political organization, although there was another force rising in Virginia politics vying for power: Bishop James Cannon.

A native of Salisbury, Maryland, Cannon was raised in a strict Methodist home and attended Randolph-Macon College in Ashland with hopes of becoming a lawyer. While a student at Randolph-Macon in the 1880s, he experienced an intense religious conversion at a tent revival that changed the course of his life and, arguably, Virginia history. Instead of heading for law school, he enrolled at Princeton Theological Seminary. He was admitted to the Virginia Conference of the Methodist Episcopal Church South and then took several jobs as pastor at congregations across Virginia.

Bishop James Cannon was a fanatical Methodist prohibitionist, a man some considered a Carrie Nation in clerical garb. Renowned for his skill and combativeness, Cannon became a founding member of the Anti-Saloon League, an organization that pressed for abolition of the demon alcohol from public life in Virginia. It was essentially a political action committee supporting so-called dry candidates who would vote for laws against the saloon and then support enforcement efforts to root out business activities of a group he called "drunkard makers."

"The way for the League to secure legislation is to go out into the field and work," Cannon said in Richmond during one of the organization's first conventions in 1902. "The League should make an active effort to enlist the press on its side."[60]

Cannon combined cutting commentary with never-ending lobbying pressure, a combination that made him one of the most dominant forces in Virginia politics during the early 1900s. One of his key allies in the House of Delegates was Richard Evelyn Byrd, Harry Byrd's father. Working with Cannon, the senior Byrd drafted bills that dried up the alcohol business in rural Virginia by 1908. Then he switched gears a bit, abandoning the progressive wing of the party and instead forming an alliance with the Martin Machine in 1909. Reformers denounced Cannon as an unethical opportunist, but it was a cynical move that helped elect Senator William Hodges Mann of Nottoway County governor of Virginia.

"The most astute politician cannot explain the inconsistency of an apparent coalition between the old guard and the prohibition element, and to the ordinary voters the proposition is simply ridiculous," the *Norfolk Ledger-Dispatch* reported in 1909. "There is apparently no possible logic which reconciles the lining up of two antagonistic forces."[61]

Cannon became so powerful that he would show up on the floor of the General Assembly, sometimes even taking a seat at the Speaker's chair. He worked with Senator Walter Mapp of the Eastern Shore to draft the 1916 prohibition law. Senator Harry Byrd was a teetotaler himself, and he voted for the state prohibition law as well as the Eighteenth Amendment. But he wasn't willing to let Cannon bully him around. During the 1924 Democratic National Convention in New York City, Cannon and Byrd shared a taxi for an awkward ride through Manhattan.

"Young man, I understand that you will be a nominee for governor," Cannon said to Byrd in his imperious fashion. "You're a nice fellow and have done a great many good things. You have a fine character and all of that, but we have decided your time is not yet. We're going to elect Walter Mapp. Your turn will come next time, perhaps later than that."

That was probably the wrong thing to say to Harry Byrd. When he got back to Winchester, he told his father what the bishop told him during that taxicab ride in New York City.

"Did that son of a bitch say that to you?" the senior Byrd responded. "Now you've got to run."[62]

The campaign for governor was a vicious fight, one that played out over the sweltering summer of 1925 as voters in the Democratic primary

Harry Byrd and Water Mapp were the two major candidates running in the race to be governor in 1925. *Library of Virginia.*

selected their candidate for governor. Because of the stranglehold on electoral politics, the winner of the Democratic primary was essentially the next governor. The stakes were high, and the smears were intense.

Mapp and his friends in the Anti-Saloon League tried to portray Byrd as a demonic force in Virginia politics. Anonymous and unsigned circulars highlighted his vote against a bill that called for public school students to read the Bible every day. Byrd said that the 1924 bill was unnecessary because school trustees already had the right to require Bible reading. But that wasn't good enough for the sanctimonious wing of the Virginia Democratic Party, which also circulated anonymous and unsigned circulars highlighting his vote against a bill on prostitution. Byrd stated that the 1916 bill was unnecessary because prostitution was already illegal and that the bill would have had the unintended consequence of decriminalizing prostitution by reducing it from a felony to a misdemeanor.

"I denounce this malicious underhanded and anonymous attack on my character and standing as a church member," Byrd declared.[63]

Not to be outmaneuvered, Byrd's supporters also had their third-party attack ads. Instead of appealing to the pearl-clutching sensibilities, they took an economic approach. In a strategy that closely resembled the fight against road bonds, Byrd supporters unleashed a barrage of circulars accusing Mapp of pushing for a full-time commission whose members would be bunch of ogres eager to slap outrageous assessments on every class of property imaginable and then let out a fiendish cackle at the inability of farmers to do anything about it.

"Leaflets and paid advertisements are being distributed in each county in the state grossly misrepresenting the plan advocated and drawing unwarranted conclusions," explained Mapp. "Will anybody's taxes be increased? Yes. Otherwise it wouldn't be worthwhile to bother with an equalization board at all."[64]

Mapp lost in a landslide. Byrd carried eight of ten congressional districts, a majority that was unprecedented in Virginia politics. Mapp was able to eke out wins in Danville, Fredericksburg, Lynchburg and Roanoke. But Byrd was able to run up the numbers in Bedford, Bristol, Norfolk, Portsmouth, Richmond and Staunton. The key to his victory was the nearly unanimous verdict of voters up and down the Shenandoah Valley, creating a sense that Byrd was now one of the most popular candidates to have ever appeared on the ballot in Virginia.

"There is not the slightest doubt in the minds of political observers that his influence with the Legislature and all agencies of the State government will be conclusive. His will be the directing voice in state affairs," proclaimed the *Richmond Times-Dispatch* after his victory in the 1925 primary. "In short, Harry Byrd, if he wishes to be, will be the Thomas S. Martin of his time."[65]

Byrd did, in fact, wish to be the Staples of his time. But he ended up creating a machine that was much more dynamic and durable.

Chapter 5

PAY AS YOU GO

Harry Byrd in the Executive Mansion

Today, people view Harry Byrd as an archconservative. His legacy is dominated by his racist massive resistance to school desegregation. But his reputation when he was elected governor was just the opposite. He was viewed as a progressive Democrat. Elected at the age of thirty-eight, Byrd brought a sense of youthful optimism. He set out to build roads, develop schools and abolish useless offices—streamlining government for maximum efficiency. Essentially, he set out to use his time in office as a kind of advertising campaign for economic development in Virginia.

"In sixty days, he had put on the statute books more constructive legislation than any previous governor had got there in four years in office," wrote Douglas Southall Freeman, as Frances Strothers noted in an article titled "Youth Takes the Helm."[66]

Unfortunately for Byrd, the Executive Mansion nearly burned to the ground in early January—only days before the inauguration. The massive conflagration started from a toy sparkler and raged out of control to leave the lower floor a blackened mess littered with the ruins of priceless heirlooms. The fire lasted only half an hour, but it left quite an impact. First Lady Helen Ball Sexton Trinkle dashed into the roaring fire to save her fifteen-year-old son, burning her face, hair, arms and hands in the process. When firefighters showed up, no ladders were long enough to reach the windows.

"Hundreds of state employees watched from the upper windows of the State Office Building," the *Richmond Times-Dispatch* reported. "Some of them turned away, convinced that rescue was impossible and unwilling to witness so horrible a tragedy."[67]

Left: Harry Byrd (*left*) at his inauguration with former Governor Elbert Lee Trinkle. *Library of Virginia.*

Below: Virginia's Executive Mansion has been the home of Virginia's governors since 1913. Just before Harry Byrd was inaugurated, it was almost destroyed by fire. *Library of Virginia.*

The Jefferson Hotel became a kind of de facto Executive Mansion for Byrd when he was governor. *Library of Congress.*

The first lady survived the fire, but she was badly burned. She ended up skipping the inauguration, which must have been a difficult decision for someone in a position to oversee all the pomp and circumstance. More than a dozen wealthy Richmonders wired the governor-elect in Winchester to offer the use of their homes. But Byrd chose instead to move into the luxurious Jefferson Hotel, the capital city's most opulent accommodations. Originally opened in 1895, the Jefferson was developed by tobacco baron Lewis Ginter as the premier property in Richmond. It featured an elaborate Spanish Baroque style, and the architect later went on to design the New York Public Library. When Byrd moved in, it became a kind of de facto Executive Mansion.

"Governor Byrd's reception was attended by all who could crowd into the Jefferson," reported the *Richmond Times-Dispatch.* "There were so many, in fact, that police had to maintain open lanes for exit for the crowd who were encouraged down the receiving line by regular army colonels and other representatives of military units."[68]

The 1926 inauguration was the first to be broadcast on the radio, but that wasn't the only innovation. The new governor also set a tone by carefully crafting his image with fashion. Instead of wearing the traditional silk hat that was commonplace among governor's taking the oath of office, he chose another route. It was a decision influenced by a chance encounter with a rural constituent.

"I hope you ain't going to become a Silk Hat Harry," the constituent said, referring to a popular cartoon strip of the era.[69]

Breaking with tradition, Byrd wore a traditional frock coat. But he ditched the silk hat in favor of a derby hat, an indication that he was ostensibly a man

The 1926 inauguration of Harry Byrd as governor was the first to be broadcast on the radio. "I hope you ain't going to become a Silk Hat Harry," one constituent quipped. *Library of Virginia.*

of the people—a blue-blood man of the people with a gold-plated last name. The only time he was seen wearing a silk hat during his time as governor was when President Herbert Hoover came to Williamsburg in 1926. During part of the trip, Byrd confided to Hoover that he had purchased his first ever silk hat for the occasion.

"Well, governor, it isn't what's on your head," the president said, "it's what's in it."[70]

Swimming around in Byrd's head was a plan for roads. His first order of business as governor was to propose a 4.5 cent gas tax, which yielded about $25 million in the first two years. To oversee the landmark program, the governor tapped Henry Shirley of Maryland to be his highway commissioner. It was a high-profile job, and Shirley had already made such a name for himself in Maryland that Byrd had to deal with his fame everywhere he went.

"How is it you're got license plate number one?" a gas station attendant once asked him, according to a popular story.

When Byrd was governor, Thomas Ozlin was Speaker of the House. Ozlin and Byrd previously worked togther on a highway funding bill that avoided debt financing. *Library of Virginia.*

"Who do you think should have it?" the governor responded.

"Commissioner Shirley, of course," the attendant shot back.

"I guess you're right," Byrd concluded.

Shirley was a shrewd political player who knew how to get things done, and he had already demonstrated an ability to navigate the system in Maryland. Now it was time for him to make an even greater name for himself in Virginia. During his time in office, Virginia's roads went from being some of the worst in the country to some of the best. One of the marquee reforms during this era was seizing control of secondary roads from the counties. Byrd concluded that counties were handling them efficiently and that it was too great of a burden. So he proposed to Shirley that the state take them over.

"Are you crazy, governor?" Shirley responded.[71]

It might have seemed crazy to many people. Virginia was doubling the mileage of roads it would have responsibility for maintaining. Shirley was concerned about the financial burden, but Byrd dragged him along. It was an idea that seemed especially crazy to county leaders across Virginia, who formed an association to oppose the idea. But they acted too slowly. By the time they got to Richmond to lobby against the bill, it had already passed the House and Senate.

THE SENATE OF VIRGINIA

When Byrd was governor, Junius West was the lieutenant governor who presided over a Senate dominated by pro-organization and anti-organization Democrats. Republicans had only a handful of seats. *Library of Virginia.*

Virginia assumed control over all the road-building machinery at fair market valuation, and the transition was timed in a way to minimize any loss to capital investment from the counties. Although it may have seemed like a far-fetched idea to Shirley, Virginia's takeover of all those secondary roads ended up eliminating a great deal of duplication and waste. It also had the added benefit of eradicating a lucrative source of graft.

The plan worked. County roads improved, and Virginia didn't take on one cent of debt. Governor Byrd suggested counties spend all that money they saved on schools. Few seemed to have taken that suggestion to heart because Virginia's schools continued to flounder.

Having accomplished his goals with roads, the new governor moved on to his next big idea: tax reform. Byrd wanted to modernize what he saw as an antiquated tax system that included county, city and village taxes. Then there were property taxes, income taxes and taxes on money in the bank. Plus there were taxes on bonds, securities and personal property. Taxes on land bore a disproportionate share of the taxes, though, and local officials appraised property to be taxed, so there were massive disparities from one place to another. Property that might be taxed $1,000 in one county might be taxed $500 in another. In addition to all of that, county revenue commissioners were forced to count every cow, pig, horse and chicken.

Byrd was concerned that the tax system was a burden on farmers. His solution was creating a clear delineation between state and local taxes. The commonwealth would be funded by a gas tax, an intangibles tax and an increased tax on public utilities and railroads, which fought the plan bitterly. At the same time, Byrd also wanted to eliminate many of the nuisance taxes.

To accomplish all this, the governor needed to revise the Virginia Constitution. He tapped one of Richmond's leading lawyers, Gray Williams, to lead the commission overseeing the revision. Williams played an important role, but Byrd was a micromanager. The governor himself took an active role in editing every period, semicolon and comma. Perhaps the most important change was the prohibition against borrowing any sum larger than $1 million, a provision that was obviously close to his heart.

The legacy of Byrd's approach to debt had drastic consequences for Virginia. On one hand, it prevented the kind of spendthrift spending that burdened so many states with the endless baggage of debt. On the other hand, bonds for turnpikes, bridges and college dormitories had a higher-than-average interest rate. One of the unintended consequences of this was disastrous for Virginia schools.

"Byrd did not do as well with the schools as with the roads because there was no special fund, like the gasoline tax, that could be applied to them," explained Senator Willis Robertson. "Although I was dedicated to the pay-as-you go system, a proper distinction can be drawn between a bond issue for capital outlay for schools that can be used for half a century, whereas highways are worn out in a few years and must be bettered."[72]

Another important reform Byrd made to the Virginia system of government was the so-called short ballot, getting rid of a laundry list of elected positions in favor of having them become appointed gigs. Before Byrd was elected governor, the entire cabinet was elected, as were many other officials. Byrd argued that this made it difficult for governors because the cabinet members were more concerned with their own political fortunes and not as focused as they could be on the administration. He agreed with President Woodrow Wilson that simplifying government was a way to avoid placing every officer "upon his own dear little statue," as Byrd put it.

"The remedy is contained in the word simplification," Byrd submitted in a message to the General Assembly days after his inauguration. "Simplify your process and you'll begin to control; complicate them, and you will get further and further away from control."[73]

Byrd's solution to this was that only three positions would be elected statewide: the governor, the lieutenant governor and the attorney general. All the formerly elected statewide positions would be appointed by the governor.

"We shall soon have an end to any semblance of a popular governor in Virginia," complained Republican lawyer Henry Anderson during the Republican state convention in the summer of 1929. "The adoption of this amendment under present conditions in Virginia not only deprived the people of their right to choose servants but was a definite step in the conversion of the existing oligarchy into an autocracy, the entrenchment of the Democratic organization in control of this state regardless of the will of the people."[74]

That meant eliminating elected positions like the state treasurer, the superintendent of instruction and the commissioner of agriculture. Instead, they would be chosen by the governor. The chief consequence of this change is that it dramatically increased the power of the governor. No longer was he beholden to a cabinet full of elected officials who were looking out for their own self-interest. Now he was overseeing an administration that answered to him and him alone. The person he appointed to lead the State Compensation Board, for example, set all the salaries of local officials. That situated the governor at the head of a government that required absolute fealty or else.

"Under the old system if things went wrong the governor could always pass the buck to an elected official," explained Bill Tuck, a future governor who was a member of the House of Delegates when Byrd was governor. "After we had the short ballot he had to take the blame."

When Byrd took control of the machinery of government, Virginia had nearly one hundred bureaus, boards and departments. If the state government were a business, he concluded, it would go bankrupt. The list of elected officials included the commissioner of insurance, public printer, second auditor and motor vehicle commissioner. When questioned about the idea the plan would make the governor too powerful, he deflected criticism by reminding critics that Virginia governors are limited to a single four-year term, adding that the Senate had to confirm many of these picks. Opposition to the amendment was led by Senator George Layman of Craig County in southwest Virginia.

"I believe the Commissioner of Agriculture ought to be selected by the farmers," he said during a debate on the Senate floor in 1928. "The people of my district do not want the short ballot, and I do not believe the people of Virginia want it."[75]

Getting an amendment added to the Virginia Constitution isn't easy. It takes two different General Assembly sessions to make it happen before it goes to voters. And an election must happen between those votes, giving maximum opportunity for voters to oppose an unpopular idea. The 1926 session approved the plan with wide margins, although it faced a mounting wall of opposition in the Senate. By the time the 1928 session rolled around, a handful of senators were ready to lead the opposition. Senator Robert Gilliam of Petersburg called the amendment "reactionary and Hamiltonian."[76]

"The leader with the foresight and the courage has been found but even the most sanguine of the workers for government reform stand amazed at the celebrity with which his suggestions are being adopted by the General Assembly," the *Richmond Times-Dispatch* editorialized in 1926. "For Virginia is accomplishing in the briefest time required to amend the Constitution those reforms in government which it had been expected would consume many years and almost endless labor both political and educational."[77]

Byrd also went to work cutting back some of the undergrowth in the jungle of bureaucracy that had emerged since the turn of the century. The previous governor received a report from the Commission on Simplification, although Elbert Trinkle did little to carry out the recommendations. Byrd reworked the committee report himself, pruning down the state government as if it were an apple tree overflowing with Albemarle Pippins. More than one hundred bureaus, boards and commissions financed by forty-eight special funds were consolidated into fourteen departments.

When British Prime Minister Winston Churchill visited the Executive Mansion, Governor Byrd had to figure out how to smuggle a quart of brandy each day during Prohibition. *Library of Congress.*

"If Virginia is to operate with the efficiency approaching a great business corporation, we must concentrate responsibility," Byrd said during his inaugural speech in 1926. "Practical experience has taught me that success is only possible when responsibility is combined with authority."[78]

Perhaps one of the more unexpected accomplishments of the Byrd administration was passing an anti-lynching law, ironic considering how the racist legacy of massive resistance has overshadowed this part of his record. The bill was prompted by the tireless efforts of Louis Jaffé, editor of the *Norfolk Virginian Pilot*. After two particularly heinous incidents of white mobs killing African Americans in southwest Virginia, Jaffé launched a campaign against lynching and leveraged the power of the press to build support for a bill in the General Assembly. Fortunately for Jaffé, the state's business community recognized that the threat of mob violence was a threat to economic development.

Sadly, though, the law was never used to convict anyone. But it was certainly a major accomplishment for Jaffé, who asked the governor to help him snag a Pulitzer Prize. In a 1929 letter, Jaffé reminded Byrd that he had been reluctant about the issue until the *Virginian Pilot* pressed the issue so relentlessly that the governor decided he had to do something.

"You will recall what a nut I have been on the subject of lynching and its eradication," Jaffé wrote to Byrd in January 1929. "I have permitted myself to believe that it was the Virginian-Pilot's persistent and, for a long-time lone-handed, advocacy of making the punishment of lynchers a State responsibility, that, supplemented with my own personal representations to you, had more to do than any other single outside urging, crystalizing your own views on this subject."[79]

During his years as governor, Byrd welcomed several famous visiting dignitaries. The most difficult was British prime minister Winston Churchill, who was a heavy drinker visiting a teetotaling state. Churchill was visiting Civil War battlefields researching for his *History of the English Speaking Peoples*, and the governor needed to figure out a way to smuggle a quart of brandy into the Executive Mansion each day of Churchill's visit. Byrd called for the services of his friend John Stewart Bryant, publisher of the *News Herald*.

"Stuart, I am in a terrible fix," the governor explained. "I need you to deliver a quart of French brandy a day."

Byrd was a teetotaler, and the Executive Mansion was dry as a bone. But he apparently had no problem with others drinking around him. In fact, he clashed with prohibitionists during his term about how prohibition enforcement officers should conduct themselves. When Byrd became governor, they wore plainclothes and no uniform. This violated his sense of dignity and the trappings of official government. If enforcement agents were going to be out and about, he concluded, they should have clearly identifiable uniforms. One of the benefits of this was that the governor could sneak in brandy for the prime minister. Fortunately for the governor, his journalist buddy had a well-stocked cellar.

"Bryan promptly supplied the brandy," explains Virginius Dabney in his 1976 book, *Richmond: The Story of a City*.[80]

Churchill's visit was colorful to say the least. He wandered around the Executive Mansion in his underwear. He made endless demands on the kitchen staff, supervising their actions and dictating the time meals should be delivered. One of the dinners had to be delayed until Harry Junior could return from the store with mustard. When Churchill came across the distinguished attorney Gray Williams, the prime minister assumed he was a butler. In that infamous gravelly British bulldog accent, he demanded action from a lawyer who turned down appointments to the Virginia Supreme Court twice.

"My man, will you fetch me a newspaper?" he asked.[81]

Williams walked across the street to the Richmond Hotel, bought a copy of the *News Leader* and then returned to the Executive Mansion and delivered it to the prime minister. Churchill tipped him a quarter.

Another A-list celebrity to visit the Executive Mansion during Byrd's term as governor was Charles Lindbergh, the flying ace who gained international fame by flying solo across the Atlantic with no radar and no radio. After that first flight from Long Island to Paris, Lindbergh set out on a tour of American cities. Richmond was the eighth stop on the tour, and Richmond's new airport was packed with ten thousand spectators.

Pickpockets worked the crowd as Lindbergh landed the silver monoplane *Spirit of St. Louis* shortly before 2:00 p.m. on a crisp autumn day. The airman took the stage and formally dedicated the first building at Byrd Field, named after Lindbergh's friend and the governor's brother Richard Evelyn Byrd. Then a motorcade took him along Broad Street to the Executive Mansion, where he stayed with the governor and his family. While he was in town, Lindbergh was celebrated at a massive dinner with five hundred guests at the Jefferson Hotel. The famous aviator ace was also honored in a ceremony at the fairgrounds and lauded in the newspapers.

"In the Governor's study of the gracious official home of Virginia, Colonel Charles A. Lindbergh, America's great eagle, stood in a group of newspaper men and women, and, unmoved by the demonstration outside, quietly told them that Commander Byrd had contributed greatly to aviation," wrote Virginia Lee Cox in the *Richmond Times-Dispatch*. "For the most part we newspaper people, knowing his antipathy to answering foolish questions, confined our queries to straight facts about aviation, which he answered from a fund of knowledge and with great courtesy."[82]

Byrd got caught up in the hysteria and desperately wanted to take a ride in the famous airplane. Lindbergh was reluctant but eventually agreed, and they drove out to the primitive airport, which wasn't much more than a few hangars and a windsock. Lindbergh meticulously inspected the airplane and then climbed in the cockpit. Byrd followed him into the one-seater, wedding himself onto Lindbergh's lap.

"It must have been a miserable flight for both of them, because Byrd was beginning to put on quite a bit of weight, and the Spirit of St. Louis had no forward visibility," noted Alden Hatch. "Byrd's nose was jammed against the instrument panel in front of the pilot's seat, and he could only catch fleeting glimpses of the ground at odd angles through a side window."[83]

Another high-profile visitor when Byrd was governor was Franklin Delano Roosevelt, who was governor of New York at the time. Roosevelt was a young reformist governor who was interested in Byrd's plan to streamline government and simplify the tax system. Byrd admired how Roosevelt whizzed around in his wheelchair like a circus acrobat. Although the two men would later become bitter enemies, they formed a friendship as reformist governors of the 1920s, and Byrd returned the favor by visiting Roosevelt in Albany.

Byrd's time as governor ended with a bit of a political crisis: the 1928 presidential election. The Democrat in that race was Al Smith, the governor of New York who had the unfortunate distinction of being the first Catholic to run for president. That led to an underground campaign of vilification, especially in the South. Senator Carter Glass hit the campaign trail on behalf of Smith, but Bishop Cannon and Reverend Billy Sunday delivered fiery speeches against the Catholic candidate. Virginia ended up going Republican for the first time since Reconstruction, leading to some soul searching among the Democratic organization leaders. Smith carried only one of Virginia's ten congressional districts.

"Hoover's victory in Virginia is interpreted to mean that the Republican-Hoover-Democrat coalition will undoubtedly put a candidate in the field to oppose the Democratic gubernatorial nominee in the next election," noted the *Richmond Times-Dispatch*. "It may mean that Democratic candidates in many counties and cities for the first time will be faced by formidable opposition in contests for local office."[84]

For Democrats, the election of 1928 was a disaster. And it set the stage for an important division inside the Democratic organization in Virginia:

the choice of who should be the candidate to take on Republican William Moseley Brown. Senator Swanson wanted Patrick Drewry of Petersburg, but Byrd thought he was a weak candidate and wanted John Pollard. Byrd drove to Washington and tried to talk the senator into his position, but the two men left the meeting without coming to an agreement.

"All right," exclaimed Byrd. "You back Drewry. I'll back Pollard."[85]

It was a proxy fight between kingmakers. Swanson threw his support behind a candidate who had been in Congress for a decade and had served eight years in the Virginia Senate before that. Drewry was a lawyer and banker in Petersburg, and he served as chairman of the Economy and Efficiency Commission, which met from 1916 to 1918 when Henry Carter Stuart was the Martin Machine governor. Pollard, on the other hand, was the attorney general who criticized election law he said put too much power in the hands of the machine. Now, by 1929, he was ready to come out of retirement as someone who was viewed as independent of the machine and an extension of the Byrd administration.

"I greatly rejoice in the wonderful progress Virginia has recently made in inducing new industries to establish themselves within our borders," Pollard said in his announcement statement. "This means increased employment for our people and improved markets for our manufactured and agricultural products. It also means increased taxable values and a consequent ability to build up better schools, better roads and better public health and welfare service without increasing the burden of taxation."[86]

Drewry didn't make it all that long. He dropped out of the race and ended up endorsing Pollard. Before he made it to the general election, Pollard had to fight off a spirited challenge from Walter Mapp, the state senator who lost the primary to Byrd four years earlier. Mapp enjoyed the support of two former governors, Westmoreland Davis and Elbert Trinkle. On the campaign trail, Mapp argued that the short ballot gave too much power to the governor. Pollard essentially sidestepped the issue, arguing that voters had already decided the issue. Pollard won the primary in a landslide, but then he had to face a Republican who enjoyed support from a coalition led by Bishop James Cannon and the Anti-Saloon League. Once again, Pollard won in a landslide.

"In electing John Garland Pollard, professor of government, to be the executive in charge of State affairs, the electorate gave a vote of confidence to Governor Harry F. Byrd, the short ballot and other amendments in the new Constitution advocated by Byrd and violently attacked both in the primary and general election," declared the *Richmond-Times Dispatch*. "The landslide victory was interpreted as disapproval of the alleged efforts of Bishop James Cannon."[87]

Byrd was now the most powerful figure in Virginia politics, and he would retain that position until the day he died—and then, arguably, many years after that. His support was so strong, in fact, that people started talking about seeing Byrd in the White House.

Chapter 6

BYRD FOR PRESIDENT

Virginia's Favorite Son, the Last New Dealer

Favorite-son candidates don't usually end up in the White House, but stranger things have happened. Warren Harding was the favorite-son candidate of Ohio when he unexpectedly ended up with the Republican nomination for president in 1920. That was a fresh memory in 1932, when Harry Byrd was a successful former governor fresh off a successful term in the Executive Mansion. It's entirely likely that he didn't expect to be the nominee and that his candidacy was a subdued affair. It's also possible that the thrill of hearing the Richmond Light Infantry Blues Band burst into "Carry Me Back to Old Virginny" was enough to cast a spell over even the most unassuming of candidates.

"Byrd's campaign for the nomination was only half-hearted," concluded historian Brent Tarter. "Had he been elected president, he probably would have been more conservative than Herbert Hoover."[88]

As Democrats gathered in Chicago for the 1932 Democratic convention, Franklin Delano Roosevelt was clearly in the lead. He won eleven of the sixteen primaries that spring, sweeping all the southern contests. Roosevelt lost the Massachusetts primary to former New York Governor Al Smith, and he lost the California primary to Speaker of the House John Nance Garner. But by the time Florida held the last primary on June 7, it was clear that Roosevelt had a majority of the delegates. But that wasn't enough to win.

Victory required two-thirds of the delegates, and a coalition of anti-Roosevelt forces was conspiring to figure out a way to deny him the

Harry Byrd was a favorite-son candidate for president of the United States in 1932. *Library of Virginia.*

New York Governor Franklin Roosevelt was the clear frontrunner to get the Democratic nomination for president in 1932, but he had powerful enemies. *Library of Congress.*

nomination. The chief opposition came from Smith, who was Roosevelt's predecessor at Gracie Mansion and the 1928 Democratic nominee for president. Smith was the candidate of the Tammany Hall Machine in New York City, an organization that was particularly strong in Chicago, where Mayor Anton Cermak packed the hall with raucous Smith partisans.

The other leading candidate was Speaker of the House John Nance Garner of Texas. He had the support of William Randolph Hearst, who ran a massive newspaper empire that influenced how many people thought about politics. Garner also had the support of Senator William Gibbs McAdoo of California, who served as secretary of the treasury in the Wilson administration. Perhaps his trump card in the fight for the nomination was that his supporters could break a potential deadlock between Roosevelt and Smith.

Former Secretary of War Nelson Baker also threw his hat into the ring by announcing that he would no longer be pressing for the Democratic Party to support entering the League of Nations. Baker had been one of the leading voices for joining the international body as secretary of war in the Wilson administration. Now his willingness to abandon the cause was an indication that he was more interested in appealing to public opinion than tilting at windmills.

Several governors were also in the running, including Maryland Governor Albert Ritchie, Ohio Governor George White and Oklahoma Governor "Alfalfa Bill" Murray. Then there was former Ohio Governor James Cox, as well as Missouri Senator James Reed. Plus there was humorist Will Rogers and banker Melvin Traylor.

Above: Al Smith and Harry Byrd campaigned with each other in 1928. By 1932, the relationship had soured. *Library of Virginia.*

Left: Speaker of the House John Nance Garner campaigns for president aboard a train. *Library of Congress.*

The reason for the explosion of candidates was that the election of 1928 had been a disaster for the party, leading to plotting and scheming among those who wanted to secure the nomination and take the party in a different direction. The candidacy of Al Smith, New York's wet and Catholic governor, had badly damaged the party in the previous election cycle. The combative Bishop James Cannon used his position in the

Left: Maryland Governor Albert Ritchie was one of the favorite-son presidential candidates in the 1932 campaign. *Library of Congress.*

Right: North Carolina Governor Oliver Max Gardner was recruited to run for governor by people who were trying to stop Franklin Roosevelt from securing the nomination. *Library of Congress.*

Methodist Church and the Anti-Saloon League to viciously attack Smith, whom he saw as a moral danger and a religious threat. On Election Day, Virginia ended up casting its lot with a Republican for the first time since Reconstruction.

Almost as soon as Byrd left the Executive Mansion in 1930, his friends were encouraging him to seek the nomination to run for president. But he and his brothers had just purchased several new apple orchards, and he was busy overseeing organization candidates in the election of 1931. So he waved off the entreaties for the time being. But after his candidates strengthened his hold on Virginia politics, the former governor began working behind the scenes to prevent the National Committee from taking a vote on the issue of prohibition. Byrd also started sizing up the field of candidates.

He invited FDR to Rosemont, the historic estate in Berryville he bought after leaving the Executive Mansion. Over lunch, the two governors talked about the danger Smith could pose to the party if he were to secure the nomination again. As news of the Roosevelt-Byrd meeting echoed around political circles, rumors began circulating that the two might end up on the ticket together. Roosevelt's chief of staff, Louis Howe, even told Byrd's brother that Roosevelt wanted Byrd on the ticket with him in 1932.

In reality, though, Byrd was already scheming to prevent Roosevelt from securing the nomination. Along with Democratic Party chairman John Raskob, Byrd devised a plan to persuade enough favorite-son candidates to create a firewall against allowing FDR to build an insurmountable lead. The first recruit was North Carolina Governor Oliver Max Gardner, who would later serve as treasury secretary in the Truman administration.

Meanwhile, Byrd also devised a convoluted plan of action that would have the General Assembly pass a resolution endorsing him for president, then he would refuse the endorsement. The idea was that this would free him up to be a mediator who would resolve conflicts in the party. Members of the General Assembly dutifully complied, passing a resolution stating that people "have lost faith in the ability of present leaders to guide in the recovery of economic prosperity and the restoration of confidence."

"While both parties at present are sadly lacking in efficient, progressive and vigorous leadership, Byrd has a genius for leadership, is simple in taste, democratic in manner and is firm and resolute in action," declared Senator Cecil Connor of Leesburg. "In point of brains, character, patriotism and accomplishment, Byrd is the peer of other governors mentioned for the presidency and in addition would be free from factional dispute."[89]

One week later, Roosevelt announced his candidacy. A few days later, Newton Baker signaled that he would run. By February, Al Smith had thrown his hat into the ring. The flurry of announcements caused Byrd to rethink his plan. Instead of refusing the endorsement from the General Assembly, he decided to accept it and establish the Virginia Byrd Committee. Governor John Pollard would serve as chairman. William Reed, president of the Larus and Brothers Tobacco Company, would be the chief financial backer. *Richmond News Leader* reporter Roy Flannagan would manage the committee.

"Virginia will be for Byrd at Chicago until he is nominated or until it is recognized that he cannot be nominated," Virginius Dabney wrote in the *New York Times*. "During his four years in office, the industrial and cultural interests of the State were advanced in phenomenal fashion and the reforms he instituted have been widely imitated. He is only 43 years old and has a dynamic personality and a remarkable gift for handling men."[90]

Byrd himself remained largely silent, hoping that the effort would be seen as something that was driven by his friends instead of himself. Ideally, that would allow him to maintain good relations with the anti-Roosevelt people and the pro-Roosevelt people. It was also a style of Virginia politics that

Part of Byrd's campaign for governor was the "resubmission plan," featured in this cartoon; it involved a complicated scheme for resubmitting the question of prohibition to voters. *Library of Virginia.*

developed during the Martin Machine—the organization would give the "nod" to the candidate that was viewed as the most likely to win.

"Transferring this provincial technique to the national scene was a risky strategy," noted historian Brent Tarter. "But he thought he might have a chance because the field was undoubtedly wide open."[91]

The issue of prohibition continued to haunt the party, and Byrd feared that it would undermine the Democrats again in 1932. So, he devised a ridiculously complicated plan that involved a constitutional amendment to change how constitutional amendments are ratified, taking it out of the power of the states and instead providing for a national referendum. That would take the heat off elected officials, who could say they have a moral responsibility to do whatever the voters demand.

"Byrd, who almost never drank, was clearly straddling the issue," explained Tarter. "His major objective was to prevent a rupture in the party, but he must have anticipated that if his plan were well received, he would be a stronger contender for the nomination."[92]

Roosevelt swept most of the presidential primaries in the months leading up to the convention in Chicago, although he lost Massachusetts to Smith and California to Garner. By the beginning of June, it was clear that Roosevelt would enter the convention with most delegates, but this wasn't enough to win. Securing the nomination required two-thirds of the delegates, and party leaders became increasingly concerned over the prospect of a deadlocked convention.

Byrd picked up the pace of the campaign, making plans to address the Women's Club of Philadelphia and the Kansas Democratic Convention. He worked with former Russell County Clerk of Court Everett Randolph Combs, who had managed his campaign for governor in the Fighting Ninth Congressional District. Now he was forming a closer relationship with Byrd that would eventually become the machinery that made the organization such a powerful force in Virginia politics for the next half century. During the 1932 presidential campaign, Combs became the tactician for the nascent Byrd Machine.

"I wish you would write letters and send them to all parts of the state urging that the county conventions endorse me," Byrd wrote to Combs in April 1932. "Of course, do not say that I have asked you to do this.... Simply say that you think it would be a nice compliment if the county conventions would endorse me when they meet."[93]

Combs planned a flawless Virginia Democratic Convention, which met at the Mosque Theater in Richmond on June 9, 1932. Members of the

The Congress Hotel in Chicago was the scene of the 1932 Democratic convention. *Library of Congress.*

convention instructed delegates to the national convention to vote for Byrd under the unit rule, essentially giving him complete control over their votes for as long as he wished. The convention adopted a platform that aligned with Byrd's critique of the Hoover administration, calling it out for deficit spending, tariff policies and the severity of the Depression.

"We want no Fascism, Communism, Sovietism or governmental collectivism in this country," Byrd said in his speech to the convention. "The Democratic party is agreed that America needs more business in government and less government in business."[94]

By the time delegates arrived in Chicago for the convention, the city was buzzing with rumors of trades and deals. Byrd set up his headquarters in Congress Hotel. The candidate's famous brother, Admiral Byrd, was there. So was General Billy Mitchell, the father of the U.S. Air Force. The Byrd headquarters also had its fair share of star power, including boxing champion Gene Tunney and humorist Will Rogers.

"Talked with Governor Byrd of Virginia," Rogers observed, "a very high-class man, which is practically his only handicap."[95]

As the convention opened, Roosevelt had a clear majority of the delegates. He was in the catbird's seat, although he didn't have enough to secure the nomination just yet. The platform was generally liberal, although not over the top. It promised to use the power of the federal government to help people struggling during the Depression. On the issue of prohibition, Byrd's convoluted compromise position was totally forgotten. Instead, the platform was unequivocal in calling for an end to prohibition and a repeal of the Eighteenth Amendment.

As Byrd and his lieutenants made the rounds, they were able to reap the benefits of the Virginia Byrd Committee. They could count on votes from North Carolina, Iowa, Mississippi and Tennessee. Byrd was also building support in the Oklahoma delegation, where Governor "Alfalfa Bill" Murray was a colorful favorite-son candidate. His campaign slogan was "Bread, Butter, Bacon and Beans," and his campaign song was "Hoover Made a Soup Hound Outta Me."

Behind the scenes, Roosevelt's people were quietly offering the vice presidency to any of the favorite-son candidates who would be the first to join the team. None was willing to take the deal, hoping that Roosevelt would crumble after three or four ballots. The nominating speeches began on Thursday, June 30, starting with Roosevelt, Garner and Smith. Delegates took a break for dinner, and then Senator Carter Glass delivered the nominating speech for Byrd.

The most colorful favorite-son candidate for president was Oklahoma Governor "Alfalfa Bill" Murray. His campaign slogan was "Bread, Butter, Bacon and Beans," and his campaign song was "Hoover Made a Soup Hound Outta Me." *Oklahoma Historical Society.*

"I present for your consideration as the nominee of the Democratic Party the most virile and accomplished governor that Virginia has had in three quarters of a century," exclaimed Glass. "At no time in the history of our government has there been greater need than now for a real man in the White House in Washington."[96]

When Glass finished the speech, the Richmond Light Infantry Blues Band marched onto the floor and played a series of songs including "Dixie" and "Yankee Doodle." The finale was, of course, "Carry Me Back to Old Virginny." The demonstration went on for

Virginia Senator Carter Glass nominated Harry Byrd for president, calling him "the most virile and accomplished governor that Virginia has had in three quarters of a century." *Library of Congress.*

more than twenty minutes, including placards that summarized the Byrd narrative: "No New Taxes," "No Deficit in Depression" and "Byrd Gave Virginia a Model State Government." White carrier pigeons were released from crevices in the roof. Colonel William Bullitt Fitzhugh, the carnation-wearing sergeant-at-arms to the Virginia House of Delegates, used a heavy cane to keep the main aisle clear.

"I've never seen a nomination demonstration change a single vote on the convention floor," quipped an obviously jealous "Kingfish" Huey Long of Louisiana.[97]

Byrd's demonstration went on for more than twenty minutes. But that was only one of the demonstrations for one of the candidates. The speeches and cheering went on all night long and well into the early morning hours in what Roosevelt campaign manager Jim Farley called a "merciless and unholy flood of oratory."[98]

The last nomination happened after 4:00 a.m., and the first roll call happened at 4:30 a.m. It took more than an hour and a half because of deep divisions in the New York delegation. Roosevelt received 666¼ votes. That was a solid majority, although not the supermajority needed. Byrd received all 24 votes from Virginia and 1 vote from the intractably divided Indiana delegation. The favorite sons were hoping that Roosevelt's candidacy would collapse after a few ballots, although the Roosevelt team was ready to rumble. Balloting went on until 9:16 a.m., when the weary but stubborn delegates wobbled out of the convention hall in search of breakfast and sleep.

The Friday night session was all right for fighting, as delegates regrouped to finish the brawl. After a fair amount of noise and animosity, the California delegation finally began the move toward Roosevelt. The tension broke, and delegates realized that they were present for the creation of a candidate. Byrd released his votes. Before the balloting had been finalized, Byrd received a telegram from Roosevelt thanking him for his support.

"Under leadership of Franklin D. Roosevelt, I am sure the Democratic Party will win a great victory in November," exclaimed Byrd. "Every possible effort on my part will be exerted to that end."[99]

Byrd was part of the committee that escorted Roosevelt to the rostrum, sitting behind FDR as he delivered his famous speech promising "a New Deal for the American people." After returning to Rosemont, he issued a statement interpreting the platform as a cautious alternative to Hoover's tariff policy. At this point, he remained optimistic about Roosevelt because he was cooperative and friendly. That would change in the coming years as the two men would form opposite ends of the Democratic Party.

"For a man as wed to economic orthodoxy as Byrd, the New Deal was thoroughly unacceptable; the plethora of alphabet agencies and constant interference of the government with the business activities of the nation were anathema to him," wrote historian Brent Tarter. "Little wonder, then, knowing as he did the temper of the times and the unpredictability of Franklin D. Roosevelt, that in 1932 he lent his support to the attempt to deny the presidential nomination to the one candidate who had within him the seeds of modern liberalism."[100]

Byrd liked to call himself "the last New Dealer," by which he meant he believed he was holding firm to the 1932 platform when others were abandoning it. By the end of Roosevelt's first 100 days in office, Byrd had abandoned FDR and the New Deal.

Chapter 7

UNION BUSTING

Byrd Machine Senses Opportunity in the Right to Work

These days, the Byrd machine is known mainly for massive resistance and pay-as-you-go spending. But there's another very significant legacy of the year's Harry Flood Byrd spent at the top of the power structure in Virginia: right to work.

The phrase "right to work" is controversial among labor groups. Opponents like to call it the "freeloader law" because it prevents employers from compelling their workers to pay union dues. That means that people who are not members of the union and don't pay dues end up getting all the advantages of being represented by the union. Business groups love the idea that unions don't really exist in Virginia, at least not in states that adopted so-called right-to-work laws back in the 1940s.

The history of how Virginia became a right-to-work state traces back to the 1940s and is a story of power politics. It culminated with the Byrd Machine governor threatening to draft union members. At the center is the hard-charging and roughhewn Governor Bill Tuck of Halifax. Tuck spent time in the House of Delegates and state Senate before becoming lieutenant governor and waiting for his turn at the Executive Mansion. Although he played the traditional game of setting himself up for the job, leaders of the machine apparently were not enthusiastic about handing him the keys to power.

"In the early years of his political life some organization leaders regarded him as a playboy and a clown who could never be trusted with the responsibility of high office," wrote J. Harvie Wilkinson. "One insider reported that Senator Byrd was a bit wary of Tuck until his election as governor."[101]

Left: Hard-charging and roughhewn Governor Bill Tuck of Halifax spent time in the House of Delegates and state Senate before becoming lieutenant governor and waiting for his turn at the Executive Mansion. *Library of Congress.*

Below: William Mumford Tuck was raised in a large family on Buckshaol Farm near Omega in Halifax County. *Virginia Department of Historic Resources.*

Tuck was harsher than most of the machine leaders, who appreciated the value of moderation. The 235-pound governor described Democratic national leadership as "political rapscallions," and he castigated opponents as "Washington wastrels" and "union churls." He railed against "Judas-like betrayals" and "outbursts of perfidy." He once declared that an organization opponent had "retracted like a man in a patch of sneeze weed." Friends liked to joke that he was "most likely to secede."[102]

William Mumford Tuck was raised in a large family on Buckshaol Farm near Omega in Halifax County. His namesake grandfather served in Company K of the Third Virginia Infantry, which fought in Pickett's Charge at the Battle of Gettysburg. Tuck's father owned a tobacco warehouse and "became the aunty's foremost tobacco chewer shortly after his twelfth birthday."[103]

He attended the College of William and Mary before leaving school to work as a principal then served in the Marine Corps before earning a law degree from Washington and Lee University. He was admitted to the bar and started practicing in South Boston. While still in his twenties, he was elected to the House of Delegates and launched a political career that would make him one of the most popular statewide politicians in Virginia history.

After he was elected to the state Senate in 1931, Tuck became part of the Byrd Machine. Tuck was more receptive to the New Deal program that was buzzing through Washington in those years. Byrd was famously hostile to Franklin Roosevelt, but there was Tuck, hitting the campaign trail for him in 1936. Two years later, though, he was denouncing the New Deal as a "wild orgy of spending."[104]

Trash talking the New Deal was a good career move for Tuck, who set himself up as a leading contender to receive the Byrd Machine's nod for the Democratic nomination for governor in 1941. But Byrd was reluctant to throw his support behind the flamboyant senator. The head of the machine was famously bland, while Tuck had a legendary outsized personality. One Richmond newspaper explained that he was "known to chew tobacco, drink whiskey, and play a wicked hand of poker....His vocabulary began where the resources of Mark Twain left off."[105]

Instead of giving the nod to Tuck in 1941, Byrd turned to Colgate Darden, a former House of Delegates member from Southampton who was currently serving in Congress. Tuck received the runner-up prize, though, in the nomination for lieutenant governor. All he had to do was preside over a bunch of state Senate sessions and the nomination would be his. By the end of Darden's time in the Executive Mansion, the governor threw his support behind Tuck. Byrd may have been reluctant to give Tuck the keys to the

In 1941, the Byrd Machine gave the nod to Colgate Darden, a former member of the House of Delegates from Southampton who became a member of Congress. *Library of Virginia.*

kingdom, but his machine wasn't. Tuck got the nomination in 1944 and beat Republican Lloyd Landreth with a whopping 67 percent of the vote.

The new governor didn't waste any time going on the offense against the labor movement, which had been growing in strength across the country for some time. Back in the early 1930s, Governor John Pollard had to send the state militia to quell a violent strike at Dan River Cotton Mills. Even as Tuck was assuming the reins of power, employees of Richmond were attempting to form a union. In his first message to members of the General Assembly, Tuck called on lawmakers to declare unionization of state and local employees in violation of Virginia's public policy. He pressed for a joint resolution that would prevent public officials from negotiating with any union of public employees—or even recognizing them as representatives in any way.

"Such an intolerable situation is utterly incompatible with sound and orderly government," the governor told a joint session of House and Senate members. "It constitutes a threat to state sovereignty."[106]

Lawmakers responded positively to the idea, bursting into applause when the new governor called on them to take action against public-sector unions.

They weren't the only ones cheering on Tuck. Newspaper editorial boards across Virginia praised the move as an effective way to combat the specter of unionism. Atlanta Mayor William Hartsfield wrote to the governor to explain that his approach was a patriotic response to the threat posed by collective bargaining.

"It seems that the radicals, pinks, Communists, extreme liberals and their fellow travelers are having a field day in this country, and everywhere people are complaining about cowardly and gutless public officials who are putting up with their crackpot ideas," Hartsfield wrote Tuck in January 1946. "Unless a line is drawn somewhere…I am afraid we are going to lose a lot of our fundamental American liberties by pure default and cowardice."[107]

Reaction from labor leaders was hostile. The leader of the effort to unionize Richmond public employees, Rex Kildow, announced that the group had decided to unionize despite the fact that Tuck and the Byrd Machine were aligned against them. Virginia Congress of Industrial Organizations regional director Ernest Pugh worried that Virginia would end up being a precedent for other states to suppress labor rights, and he described Tuck's message to lawmakers as "a vicious anti-labor message." He blamed the man at the head of the machine for Tuck's assault on unions and unionism.

"Byrd is jerking the strings by which Tuck dances," said Pugh. "The CIO deplores the governor's announced policy and feels that he is adopting the same tactics that were adopted by Hitler and Mussolini."[108]

Comparing the governor to fascist dictators didn't go over well in the General Assembly.

"I resent bitterly that statement, and I'll be damned if I am going to see a statement like that published in the press without taking advantage of my rights to take exception," said Delegate Frank Moncure of Stafford.[109]

Tuck's resolution passed the General Assembly in short order, and lawmakers added several other measures. One prohibited the use of violence, which had been a problem in the early 1930s during a strike at the Dan River Cotton Mills. The General Assembly responded by adding a new requirement that all members of a picket line be employees of the company that was the target of the strike. Another addition prohibited the state from rehiring any employee who participated in a strike for two years. Labor leaders were worried this was laying the groundwork for prohibiting all collective bargaining, regardless of whether it happened in the public sector or in private business. Meanwhile, in Washington, Senator Byrd introduced legislation in Congress requiring unions to register with the Securities and

Aeroplane View by "Liberty Flyers."

NEW RIVERSIDE COTTON MILL, DANVILLE, VA.

Above: Dan River Cotton Mills had been the scene of a labor dispute that turned violent, creating a new sense of urgency as more labor unrest grew in the 1940s. *Virginia Historical Society.*

Left: This Neoclassical building in Richmond was the original headquarters for the Virginia Electric Power Company, known as VEPCO. *Virginia Historical Society.*

Exchange Commission. "Unions should be held to the same accountability as would be done in the case of an individual or corporation," said Byrd.[110]

Tension between the governor and labor leaders came to a blistering climax during a confrontation with workers of the Virginia Electric and Power Company, a utility known as VEPCO that was the forerunner to the modern-day political powerhouse Dominion Energy. The organization traces its corporate roots back to 1787, when the General Assembly authorized the creation of the Appomattox Trustees to extend navigation on the Appomattox River. By the mid-1940s, VEPCO was providing power to more than half of Virginians.

At the beginning of 1946, VEPCO employee members of Richmond and Norfolk locals of the International Brotherhood of Electrical Workers were trying to get the National Labor Relations Board to fix bargaining units. Union leaders said that salaries had not kept pace with other industries, and they believed that VEPCO had violated a contractual obligation made in 1941 to increase salaries 20 percent to 25 percent. They were trying to get federal regulators to take action against VEPCO, but they didn't seem to be getting anywhere.

"We feel that if NLRB had done what was right, we would have a new and better contract now," said George Colonies, president of Local B-1064 in Richmond. "The indefiniteness of the situation holding up our negotiations for a new contract must be dealt with immediately."[111]

Colonies was frustrated the NLRB was "too doggone slow," as he put it, although its sluggishness was understandable. Any action it took in the Virginia case would be seen as a precedent for other states. Eventually, union leaders grew tired of waiting for the federal agency to take action. So they announced that they would suspend work on January 25, a threat they hoped would force a decision from the NLRB on salaries as well as a separate issue clarifying that foremen, plant clerks, chemists and meter readers were eligible for membership. Union leaders backed down when federal officials called for a special hearing in Washington on January 31.

When the NLRB finally got around to issuing a formal decision on March 4, none of the issues was resolved. The board didn't decide the salary issue, and it didn't make a ruling on who was eligible for union membership. That led to an impasse in contract negotiations, and the two sides became involved in a bitter stalemate. Union leaders filed a formal notice that 1,800 workers would be striking unless they were able to negotiate a new contract. That would have meant a blackout for sixty-three counties in Virginia and sixteen in North Carolina and four in West Virginia.

"This is just as bad as Jesse James or Dillinger," Tuck said in a private meeting. "It's just like sticking a gun in your back. And they'll not get by with it as long as I'm governor."[112]

The governor wasn't about to let that happen. So he tried to set up a meeting with union leaders and company representatives to see if he could resolve the issue. But union officials said that they would not meet unless the governors of North Carolina and West Virginia were part of the meeting too. Tuck wasn't about to agree to that, so instead he announced that Virginia would seize and operate the utility to head off the strike.

"This is a drastic step. So far as I am able to learn, it is also unprecedented," Tuck said in a written statement. "I appeal to the people of Virginia to stand firm with me in my efforts to safeguard the welfare of all. I trust and believe they will."[113]

Even as the unions were setting up strike committees and selecting picket captains, the governor and his team were plotting a strategy to use the Virginia State Guard, an emergency militia unit formed during World War II. The unit was to be disbanded at the end of the war, but Governor Colgate Darden extended the service of the outfit until June 30, 1946. Battalion guards told reporters they were alerted the governor might call them into service to handle the strike. The adjutant general, Samuel Gardner Waller, tried to persuade journalists to conceal that development from the public.

"To newspapermen, General Waller said he did not think information concerning the possible use of the guard should be made public," the *Times-Dispatch* reported on its front page.[114]

Tuck certainly had the element of surprise on his side when he asked VEPCO for a list of essential employees. The company supplied the list, even though the governor declined to explain why he asked for it. VEPCO President Jack Holtzclaw said that he would not oppose the governor's power to seize its properties and equipment to avoid an interruption of service. Tuck then declared a state of emergency and mobilized three thousand members of the Virginia State Guard assembled at their armories. Any connection between these two developments was not yet apparent.

"Governor Tuck declined last night to discuss the guard mobilization," explained the *Richmond Times-Dispatch*. "The full import of the guard mobilization may be made clear by an emergency proclamation expected from the governor today."[115]

Tuck was finally able to spring his surprise at 9:00 a.m. the morning of Friday, March 29. The reason he needed to mobilize all those state guardsmen is so they could serve draft notices to 1,500 VEPCO workers, which started promptly at the start of the workday that morning. He was invoking an obscure section of the military code declaring all able-bodied males between the ages of eighteen and fifty-five as privates in the state militia. The governor, acting as commander in chief of Virginia's military, issued two executive orders that morning: one inducting all VEPCO employees into an organized militia and another suspending active military duty, a suspension that would be lifted in the event of a strike. It was, in the words of one historian, "the most dramatic, albeit unorthodox, service of its career."[116]

Instead of seizing VEPCO properties and equipment, Tuck's artful solution to the problem was to essentially seize the VEPCO workers instead. By placing them under military law, VEPCO workers would be subject to a court-martial if they refused to work for Virginia in the event of a strike. The goal was to prevent a violation of the state's public utility law, which a VEPCO strike would have been under the governor's logic. The maximum penalty under the military code would be a $200 fine or two hundred days in jail. The militia was designated the "Emergency Laws Executing Unit," and it was ordered to make sure VEPCO continued to provide electric service.

"The lights in Virginia will not go off," declared Tuck. "I am not at this time trying to solve any social, economic or labor problems. They can be solved in the weeks, months and years ahead. I am simply exercising my duties and the powers of the high office which I hold to see that suffering, death and devastation to not come to Virginia."[117]

A detail of twenty-five guardsmen from the Third and Fourth Battalion was briefed at the Blues Armory at Sixth and Marshall Streets and then served notices at the Twelfth Street power station before moving on to other stations and substations. The detail was divided into three-man groups of guards that would go through each plant with escorts of foremen and supervisors. Only a few VEPCO employees refused to accept the draft orders, although National Guardsmen read them aloud anyhow. These defiant union workers were warned that if they did not report to a designated officer within twenty-four hours, they would be considered AWOL.

"I don't believe this is legal. The Navy hasn't released me yet," responded one worker, scratching his head in disbelief. "I don't believe I can be in the Army and the Navy at the same time."[118]

When a newspaper reporter told one worker to frame the notice because it was signed by the governor, he cracked, "If I do, I'll hang it in my privy."[119]

The head of the American Federation of Labor said that it was involuntary servitude, complaining that VEPCO employees were essentially working a chain gang and comparing the governor's actions to something

The Blues Armory at Sixth and Marshall Streets in Richmond served as the headquarters of the military takeover of VEPCO. *Library of Virginia.*

that would have happened in Fascist Italy. The head of the Food, Tobacco and Agricultural Workers said that the governor's actions were a threat to the democratic principles of collective bargaining. Frantic VEPCO workers assembled at Murphy's Hotel at the corner of Broad and Eighth Streets in Richmond, many angry and willing to brave a potential court-martial.

"The most sinister, damnable and unprincipled act to date coming from the high command of Byrdism," is how Virginia CIO Council President Boyd Payton described the maneuver. "We believe it would be impossible to find any organization, political or otherwise, that could more rightly be labeled an organization of evil leadership than that of the political organization of the Byrd machine."[120]

In the event that the drafted workers were to be enlisted into active duty, they would have been entitled to a base pay of fifty-one dollars per month, a detail that hadn't really been thought through by the penny-pinching governor, who said the details of all that were still being worked out. He didn't have an estimated cost for the plan because it was never really meant to be carried out. It was designed to force the union to stand down.

"If the workers are to be compelled in peacetime to work and fight against their own interests, then democracy is at an end in Virginia," proclaimed E.L. King, president of the Norfolk Central Labor Union, in a telegram to

Left: Murphy's Hotel at the corner of Broad and Eighth Streets in Richmond became the gathering spot for angry VEPCO employees willing to brave a court-martial. *Library of Congress.*

Opposite: President Harry Truman took a page out of Tuck's playbook by threatening to draft railroad workers into the armed forces. *Library of Congress.*

the governor. "Unless you and the owners of the Virginia Electric and Power Company recall your dictatorial order, every laborer in Virginia will take necessary steps to make ineffective your dictatorial action."[121]

Union leaders were outraged. But the business community approved.

"The people of Virginia are getting sick and tired of being pushed around by strikes here and strikes there with the ensuing discomforts and economic adversity because of the inability of employer and employee to agree on terms of employment," the *Danville Bee* editorialized. "Perhaps Governor Tuck has found a prescription for the wave of costly strikes at all events, strikes which affect the public service."[122]

As it turns out, Tuck's gamble paid off. The International Brotherhood of Electrical Workers called off the strike late in the day on March 30, announcing that they would resume negotiations. That led to two more weeks of bargaining, culminating in a new contract guaranteeing each worker a wage increase of at least fifteen cents per hour. VEPCO agreed to set up a fund to eliminate inequalities in its wage structure, a provision designed to increase wages for some employees by as much as thirty cents an hour. But there was a catch: no strikes during the course of the agreement.

Although labor leaders were unhappy with Tuck's maneuver, the Virginia public was apparently thrilled. Letters and telegrams flooded into the Executive Mansion in support of the governor's executive action thwarting union power. A look through Tuck's gubernatorial papers shows many letters of support. They included elected officials and regular citizens.

"What the nation needs is not only a good 5-cent cigar, but 47 more governors like Governor Tuck," exclaimed Southside resident Benjamin

Mears, adding that the governor "has the fortitude to stand up for all the people and not only for the barons of organized labor."[123]

Tuck took office under a cloud, the perception that he was a lightweight. But the VEPCO affair showed that he could play hardball, and the move transformed his standing in the Byrd Machine. He could have used his newfound celebrity to become the poster child for the anti-labor movement. Instead, though, he expressed concern for the workers. Writing to Senator

Byrd, Tuck concluded that the episode showed the need for legislation setting up a new system of dispassionate arbitration.

"I think unquestionably Virginia will have to pass laws enabling employees of public utilities to settle," the governor wrote to the senator in July. "Their disputes are before some board which would be fair to them."[124]

The VEPCO affair was the most prominent labor dispute in Virginia, but it was only one in a long parade of labor disputes unfolding that year across the country. After the conclusion of World War II, prices soared, and organized labor demanded a slice of the pie. From meatpackers and steel workers to coal miners and railroad engineers, the late 1940s were an era of unprecedented labor unrest. President Harry Truman even ended up taking a page out of Tuck's playbook by threatening to draft railroad workers into the armed forces.

"The action taken by Governor Tuck is nearly identical with the action now proposed by the president," Senator Byrd said in a speech on the Senate floor. "In Virginia, the strike was stopped and no further trouble has occurred."[125]

Having created the template for using the brute force of executive power to kneecap labor unions, Tuck was ready to chart a legislative path for undermining them indefinitely. At the end of the year, he called a special session ostensibly about education. But as lawmakers arrived in Richmond in January 1947, it was clear that they would also be taking action on a plan that would change the face of Virginia history—a proposal he called a "right to work" bill. In his address to lawmakers at the beginning of the session, he sold the idea as a way to preserve the liberty of the working man.

"It would ensure that his right to earn a livelihood for himself and his family would not be dependent upon the whims of an arbitrary, unscrupulous or despotic union leadership," said Tuck. "If our system of government, with all its blessings, is to survive, the existing economic dictatorship imposed by ruthless union leaders must be curbed."[126]

A public hearing on the labor bills packed the House chamber beyond capacity, cramming people onto the floor, into the aisles and spilling out into the lobby and filling the balcony with spectators. The *Richmond Times-Dispatch* noted that old-timers about the Capitol estimated it was "the largest crowd ever to attend such an event." Each side was given one and a half hours to speak for or against the bills, leading to a raucous hearing that was punctuated by booing of speakers on both sides.

"Will you maintain order?" asked Senator Robert Norris of Lancaster, who was presiding over the joint meeting to the House and Senate committees considering the legislation. "Or shall I clear the gallery?"[127]

If the real problem was a disruption of public utilities service, critics argued, then why wasn't any effort made to investigate that issue? Nobody was suggesting anything like that, nor was anybody proposing a plan to broaden the powers of the State Department of Labor and Industry. The National Labor Relations Board had already declared that VEPCO and Appalachian Power violated the National Labor Relations Act, and yet nobody was forcing them to include arbitration clauses in new contracts. Instead, the conversation was focused on a so-called right-to-work bill, which CIO director Ernest Pugh suggested should be called "a bill to launch Virginia into the union-busting business."

"Labor is on the whipping block," declared Joseph McIntosh, international representative of the International Brotherhood of Workers, adding that the governor's proposals "are the answer to the utilities fondest prayer."[128]

Unsurprisingly, business interests lined up to speak in support of the bills. Supporters included the Virginia Farm Bureau Federation and the Peninsula Association of Commerce, as well as individual businesses, including the Blue Buckle Overall Company and the Old Dominion Box Company. They argued that that citizen had an interest in keeping their public utilities running and that labor unions were a form of "involuntary servitude."

"We can't close down these power plants," argued Richmond lawyer John Girsby, simply to satisfy "a few labor racketeers who cause all the trouble."[129]

The governor's bills were introduced by Delegate Edward McCue of Charlottesville, and they got out of the House Labor Committee with an eleven-to-two vote. The action was taken by an unrecorded voice vote behind closed doors, so we don't know the identity of the lawmakers who opposed the bill in committee. An editorial in the *Richmond Times Dispatch* quoted an anonymous lawmaker who voted in favor of the bill even though he told the newspaper he thought they were bad bills. But, he said, he was so disgusted with the attitude of labor leaders who made no arguments on the merits of the bill and instead threatened to send him packing in the next election.

"He has reached the considered conclusion that passage of the governor's bills may help to show the obnoxious type of labor leadership that its bulldozing and arrogant tactics will not be tolerated," the paper editorialized. "There are plenty others like him."[130]

When the right-to-work bill was considered in the House, opponents tried to amend the bill in a way that would declare open shops the public policy of Virginia, sending the issue to the Virginia Legislative Council for study. That amendment was defeated in a vote of sixty-five to twenty-seven, indicating an overwhelming majority in favor of the bill. Supporters argued that the bill was a necessary counterbalance to what they perceived as the abuses of organized labor in recent years, and they added there was no reason to sit around and wait for Congress to take action.

"This bill is designed to afford the right to work to any man, whether he pays a fee to a union or not," said Delegate Blackburn Moore of Berryville. "Of course, we all know perfectly well that unions would not be interested in having members join the union if no fee were involved. So it gets down to the matter of putting fee on the right to work."[131]

Opponents of the bill pointed out that the National Labor Relations Act governed most labor-management relations and warned that it would take precedence over any action the General Assembly took on the issue. They cited instances where the closed shop had a record of being beneficial to both employer and employee. They predicted strife and disturbances between unions, which would be in competition with one another. They warned of a flood of damage lawsuits.

"Let's not be reactionary," said Delegate Stuart Campbell of Wytheville, who led the opposition. "The only organization I know of that demands no dues from its members is the church."[132]

The House of Delegates gave the bill an overwhelming vote of approval, seventy-seven to twenty. When it made its way across the Capitol to the Senate, the chief advocate for the right-to-work bill was Senator Robert Norris of Lancaster County, who was chairman of the Committee on Courts of Justice. He argued that labor conditions were better in Virginia than in many other parts of the country.

"Even so, conditions prevailed in Virginia during the war when a man couldn't get work unless he joined a labor union," said Norris.

Senator Robert Brock of Farmville argued that the tendency to abuse power was inherent in human nature, and some kind of safeguard needed to be in place to guarantee a balance. He recalled an era that management had ruthlessly exploited labor, leading to what he viewed as a series of "damnable" appeasements.

"We have built up a colossus," said Brock. "Now it is necessary to curb labor."

Opponents of the bill acknowledged the excess of labor, and they attacked the radical labor leaders of the era. Senator James Tyler of Norfolk was one of two senators to speak on the floor against the bill, arguing that it was "ill-conceived, ill-considered and a useless gesture."

"This bill does not cure the thing you are trying to cure," said Tyler. "I am afraid it will hurt the cause of industrial peace and will leave the impression that the governor and the General Assembly hate labor."[133]

The Senate vote was even more lopsided than the one in the House. Senators approved the bill with a vote of thirty-two to six. In the House and in the Senate, support for the right-to-work law came from across Virginia. The only part of the commonwealth that had any measure of opposition was the coal mining region in the southwest, where organized labor had an outsized influence. Richmond attorney Martin Hutchinson, who had unsuccessfully challenged Harry Byrd in a primary the previous year, believed the whole point of the extra session was to crack down on labor.

"It is my impression that the session was called for the purpose of hitting at labor and in that way helping advance the national prestige of Byrd, who, of course, has presidential ambitions," said Hutchinson. "Byrd and his people know that they have lost the laboring people."[134]

It was a political calculation that paid off. For many stateside elections to come, anti-labor sentiment provided a vast reservoir of political goodwill. Writing off labor unions ended up giving the Byrd Machine a useful tool: standing in opposition to a group they portrayed as bombastic, arrogant, counterproductive and heavy-handed. In the end, Tuck's stand against labor unions ended up becoming his most significant achievement in office.

"As Tuck's personal popularity grew, so too did the strength of the Byrd organization," wrote Tuck biographer William Bryan Crawley. "By the midpoint of the Tuck governorship, the organization had established unprecedented control over the political affairs of Virginia."[135]

Chapter 8

THE YOUNG TURKS

Fresh from the War, the Greatest Generation Takes on the Machine

The Byrd Machine was never open to youth. The whole organization was built on seniority and waiting your turn, which made its chief lieutenants seem even more senior than their age. Perhaps that's why a group of House members known as the Young Turks made such a splash, pushing back against the machine from the inside rather than trying to battle it from outside the gates. Republican and anti-organization Democrats had been conspiring against the machine unsuccessfully for years.

The Young Turks offered something different and more dangerous, organization men who were concerned the pathological hatred of debt was undermining everything from education and infrastructure to governance and even the commonwealth's reputation. They were, in fact, young, especially relative to other members of the General Assembly. They were not, however, Turks, although most of them were veterans of World War II. So they had seen enough of the world to know that Harry Byrd didn't write all the rules of government. Most of them were first elected in 1947, the first election after the war. By the time they were reelected in 1949, they began to exert power.

The phrase "Young Turks" was first used during the 1950 General Assembly session. At the conclusion of the session, *Richmond Times-Dispatch* political reporter James Latimer explained the influence of this "group of energetic House sophomores" who "symbolize a new spirit of independence within organization ranks." They questioned the old pay-as-you-go philosophy, challenged racial segregation and forced a debate on the racist poll tax.

After the end of World War II, many returning veterans arrived at the General Assembly eager to shake things up. *Library of Congress.*

"The Young Turks—it's not known who put that tag on them—represented something so far as recent legislative sessions are concerned," Latimer wrote. "They generally were within the organization, yet didn't hesitate to challenge its dictums."[136]

The leader of the pack was Delegate Armistead Boothe of Alexandria, a Rhodes Scholar who got his start in politics as city attorney for Alexandria in the late 1930s and early 1940s. In 1949, he wrote an article in the *Virginia Law Review* predicting that the Supreme Court would rule segregated schools unconstitutional. During the 1950 General Assembly session, he tried to set up a nine-member commission to study race relations. He also introduced a bill repealing Jim Crow–era statutes requiring segregation on common carriers, a forward-looking proposal that presaged much of the debate over segregation that would dominate Virginia politics for the next decade.

"Is Mr. Boothe actually so naive as to believe this morsel thrown to the wolves will satisfy them or that it will lay low the threat of federal intervention?" asked Homer Gilmer Richey of Charlottesville in a letter to the editor opposing the bill. "If he feels that, as a taxpayer, he is contributing unduly to the support of white facilities, educational or otherwise, then I suggest that all state and local taxes payed by Negroes be earmarked and

Above: Delegate Armistead Boothe of Alexandria was the leader of the Young Turks. *University of Virginia Special Collections.*

Left: After his term as governor, Colgate Darden became president of the University of Virginia. He supported Armistead Boothe's proposal for integrated public transportation. *Library of Virginia.*

applied exclusively for Negro benefits. But then let us apply the same rule to taxes paid by whites."[137]

The idea that buses, trains and streetcars would be integrated was a nonstarter for most members of the General Assembly, and the strongest opposition came from parts of Virginia where the population of Black citizens outnumbered whites. But it did have one notable supporter: former Governor Colgate Darden, who was now president at the University of

Virginia. The former governor made an appearance at the Courts of Justice committee to testify in favor of Boothe's bill, giving it an official stamp of approval from a Byrd Machine governor with stellar credentials. Boothe argued that the bill was a way to sidestep aggressive federal intervention.

"Unless we make fair, slight, moderate concessions to the colored people, very shortly we may not be able to make any concessions voluntarily," Boothe told colleagues.[138]

Darden wasn't the only celebrity endorsing the idea. Supporters also included Episcopal Bishop Henry St. George Tucker and industrialist John Brockenbrough Woodward of Newport News. Opposition came from parts of Virginia with the heaviest population of African Americans: Southside, Tidewater and central Virginia. These were some of the oldest members of the General Assembly, people who represented rural communities. Supporters of Boothe's effort to desegregate public transportation and create a race commission were part of a rising new generation.

"The heaviest support for the bills came from urban lawmakers and from younger members, particularly veterans of World War II serving in the House," wrote Parke Rouse in the *Richmond Times-Dispatch*.[139]

Rouse named several members who would later be dubbed Young Turks: Armistead Boothe of Alexandria, E. Griffith Dodson of Roanoke, Julian Rutherfoord of Roanoke and George Cochran of Staunton. These were the young rising generation of the Byrd Machine—House members who were pressing for change from inside the organization rather than joining the ranks of the anti-organization Democrats or the Republicans. Two other Young Turks were making noise over in the House Privileges and Elections Committee, forcing a vote on a resolution to allow a referendum on the poll tax: Delegate Walter Page of Norfolk and Delegate Dodson of Roanoke. The Senate Privileges and Elections

The 1952 House of Delegates had many members who would later become known as Young Turks, including Armistead Boothe of Alexandria; Stuart Carter of Botetourt County, Carolina; Griffith Dodson of Roanoke; Walter Page; Julian Rutherfoord of Roanoke; and George Cochran of Staunton. *Library of Virginia.*

Committee quietly killed it with a five-to-four vote, but it was clear that this group was wielding a new sense of power in the rickety old machine. There was one issue, though, that united the Young Turks with the anti-organization Democrats and the Republicans: state spending.

That issue unexpectedly blew up at the end of the 1950 session, just as the Young Turks were coming into their own. The reason for this was Delegate Robert Whitehead, who was decidedly not a Young Turk. A veteran of World War I, Whitehead was from an earlier generation. But he was also the leader of liberals in the House, and the Young Turks were the liberal wing of the Byrd Machine.

"The last of the old-fashioned spellbinders, the Patrick Henry of his generation, Whitehead had wide support among the farmers and could speak their language," wrote historian Peter Henriques. "Yet he was also a lucid and progressive thinker with a grasp of complicated financial matters unequaled in the state."[140]

While looking over the budget, Whitehead realized that the House Appropriations Committee made a mistake. Somehow, it didn't include revenue from unexpended appropriations. That meant Virginia had an extra $2 million to spend, an unexpected windfall created by an accounting mistake. Whitehead managed to persuade the House of Delegates to add an extra $1 million for teachers, raising the salary of ten thousand teachers about $50 per year. Opponents argued that the schools had plenty of funding and adding more money would throw the budget out of balance. The vote was sixty-two to thirty-three.

But the idea didn't fare so well in the Senate, which was loaded with machine pols. The Senate added $2 million in new appropriations to the House budget, including money for a new tuberculosis facility for Black people. The Whitehead amendment adding money for schools was stricken, though, on the grounds that it would unbalance the budget. House and Senate leaders appointed a conference committee to iron out the details, which happened with lightning speed. That's because House Speaker Blackburn Moore packed the conference committee with opponents of the Whitehead amendment, even though the idea was overwhelmingly popular in the House.

"I shook the tree, but somebody else picked up the apples," complained Whitehead ruefully.[141]

Many in the House were angry and outraged about the rejection of the Whitehead amendment, including the Young Turks. The conference committee report didn't really end the debate, which dragged on until the closing hours of the General Assembly session. As the sixty-day session was drawing to a close, lawmakers were still deadlocked. As midnight approached, lawmakers engaged in the age-old trick of literally stopping the clock in the House chamber at 11:22 p.m. to prolong the session past the witching hour. A group of senators arrived in the House chamber to start twisting arms, and they soon set their sights on one of the Young Turks: Delegate Dodson of Roanoke.

"One well-known senator went so far as to warn him that his father would lose his job as clerk of the House unless Dodson switched his vote," explained historian Peter Henriques. "Such pressure simply made Dodson firmer in his opposition to the governor's budget."[142]

Governor John Battle started calling wayward members to his office one by one, personally twisting arms in a

Governor John Battle called the Young Turks into his office one by one, personally twisting arms in an effort to prevent increasing the budget for education. *Virginia Historical Society.*

series of brief but intense meetings that lasted into the morning hours. The meetings were not open to the public or the press, of course, so there is no official record of what was said behind the closed doors of the Capitol's third floor. Certainly, the Byrd Machine mantra against deficit spending was part of the discussion. It's entirely likely that the governor argued for responsibility to the organization. Perhaps Battle made the case that supporting opposition to the administration's budget would be viewed as support for the anti-organization efforts of Delegate Whitehead, who was angling for a campaign for governor.

"I've had 10 men tell me how they've been talked to on this thing," Whitehead declared as a final vote approached. "They give us all this talk about 'we don't have the money,' but they find enough money for everything they want."[143]

The session finally ended at 3:35 a.m. Teachers did not get a raise, and the coalition between the Young Turks and Whitehead was a bust. But the momentum they started continued to grow, and the themes that emerged in that 1950 session continued to be a rallying cry for the new generation of Byrd Machine insiders. Two years later, Delegate Walter Page was back with another effort to repeal the poll tax.

"Repeal of the voting tax is overdue," editorialized the *Richmond Times-Dispatch*. "The tax serves no useful purpose, and the perennial arguments over it are extremely tiresome."[144]

The Young Turks were unable to ditch the poll tax that year, but the pressure campaign was working. Machine-aligned lawmakers were starting to think about things in a new way, and editorial boards were even chiming in to agree. Lawmakers were starting to consider ways to steer more money to Virginia's underfunded schools, and the youthful spirit of the young lawmakers was infectious.

"The group, full of something akin to college spirit and often better organized than the leadership, has refused to go stand in the corner in spite of suggestions to that effect," wrote political reporter Charles McDowell in the *Times-Dispatch*. "Anybody who hasn't heard them coming has only been listening out of one corner of his ear."[145]

They would meet every night to talk, argue and plan at the Hotel Richmond, now the state-owned Barbara Johns Building. There they launched a strategy to force the old-line leadership to make substantial concessions to fiscal policy. Once again, they were pushing for increased investments in education. This time, unlike the 1950 Whitehead amendment, they were successful.

The 1954 General Assembly session was the apex of the power and prestige of the Young Turks. That was when they were able to use their

Opposite: The Young Turks wanted to eliminate the poll tax, which they viewed as an antiquated barrier to participation at the polls. But the Byrd Machine made sure that it remained part of the system as long as possible. *Library of Congress.*

Above: The Young Turks met at the Hotel Richmond, where they launched a strategy to force the old-line leadership to make concessions to their strict fiscal policy. *Library of Congress.*

influence to leverage support for an effort to suspend an automatic tax refund bill introduced by Senator Harry Byrd Jr., son of the U.S. senator who was now carrying out the machine's economic agenda in the General Assembly. The idea behind the automatic refund was that the state's $7 million surplus be returned to taxpayers, although that would have only been a few dollars for individual households. The House Appropriations Committee, which was stacked with organization stalwarts, included it in the budget its members sent to the full House.

But when it got to the House floor, Boothe and the Young Turks pushed for an amendment that spent the budget surplus on capital outlay throughout the state. Instead of returning a few dollars to households across Virginia, the Young Turks argued, it was a better idea to appropriate the money to help Virginia's crumbling schools: $2 million to increase teacher salaries in poor localities, $2 million for a new hospital at the University of Virginia, $750,000 for a new library at Old Dominion University, $167,000 for a poultry research plant and livestock center at Virginia Tech and $143,000 to modernize the power plant at the Virginia Military Institute. The debate on the House floor dragged on for five hours, culminating in a vote of fifty-two to forty-five.

"We want to face up as we should face up to the needs of Virginia," Boothe told lawmakers. "And we want to delay the death of the pay-as-you-go plan in Virginia."[146]

The Young Turks practically dared the Senate to dump the Boothe amendment. Delegate Stuart Carter of Botetourt County said if the Senate kills the amendment "let the blood be on the hand that wields the dagger."[147] Perhaps after the fifth conference committee some of the House and Senate negotiators were ready for bloodshed. The epic session stretched on until eleven o'clock on a Sunday night at the end of the General Assembly session, when lawmakers were tired and cranky and eager to return home. The final compromise called for $2.2 million worth of investments; some $5 million would be returned to taxpayers. The House approved the compromise, but the Senate rejected it by a vote of twenty to nineteen.

Then some major late-night legislative drama unfolded behind the scenes at the Capitol. Indignant at the Senate's rejection of the compromise, the Young Turks decided that they would simply walk out. The House would not be able to pass a budget without fifty-one votes, and the Young Turks resolved that they would not return unless the House sergeant-at-arms came after them. When word of their plan reached Senate clerk E.R. Combs, political sage of the Byrd Machine, he urged senators to accept the compromise and adjourn the session. They did what they were told, and the Senate agreed to the compromise with a vote of twenty-seven to nine.

"The main political fact of the 1954 session, evident for all to see and ponder, was the emergence of a House coalition led by the 'Young Turks,'" wrote James Latimer in the *Times-Dispatch*. "This group took and held firm control of the House through the long and bitter struggle over the budget and the Byrd income tax credit law. Thus, for the first time in many sessions, the old-time organization leaders last control of the House at crucial moments, a situation which some saw as perhaps the beginning of the end for the Byrd organization and others viewed as being only a temporary phenomenon."[148]

The Young Turks finally scored the victory they had been pushing for all along, investing in Virginia's crumbling schools. Sure, they didn't get all $7 million. But that was likely a bargaining position that allowed them to get

Everett Randolph
Combs, pictured here
with Harry Byrd, was
the clerk of the Senate
and the political sage
of the Byrd Machine.
*University of Virginia
Special Collections.*

to the $2.2 million compromise. They worked from inside the machine to change how the machine worked, steering it away from the crusty old belief that everything was fine with the schools and teachers in poor communities didn't need a raise. Governor Thomas Stanley said he thought there would be a place for the Young Turks in the organization, adding that young blood was "very much desired." Boothe could count the budget fight as a major victory and take the accomplishment on the campaign trail to campaign for the Senate.

"I think this is a very healthy thing for the state and for the organization itself. It broadens the base of the party's representation," said Boothe. "The tree of good government can flourish better if its roots are sunk more deeply in the ground and spread over a wider area, rather than being nurtured from a limited source."[149]

Anti-organization Democrats hoped that the 1954 session would be the beginning of the end for the Byrd Machine. But the Young Turks emphasized their role in the organization rather than opponents of it. Newspaper reporters portrayed Boothe as the leader of the movement, although other Young Turks did not share his views on desegregating buses or establishing a race commission.

"Most of these members considered the Young Turk revolt a one-issue effort to rectify some serious unaddressed needs," explained historian Douglas Smith. "They were not interested in taking power away from the organization."[150]

Washington Post columnist Benjamin Muse pointed out that the history of the name Young Turks dates back to a group of young men who stirred things up in Turkey in 1908 and 1909, modernizing a country that was known at the time as the "Sick Man of Europe." He pointed out that the original Young Turks were bookish and more noisy than dangerous, desperately trying to westernize a country that had been governed by brute force and ancient traditions. They reorganized the country, brought about a new constitution and created a system of electing government officials.

"The comparison so far with the Virginia situation is a bit overdrawn, but points of resemblance are there," Muse mused. "It is quite possible to recognize Armistead Boothe Pasha and Stuart Carter Effendi in that picture."[151]

Name-checking some of the original Young Turks who pushed for reform of the Ottoman Empire, Muse went on to compare their struggle against Sultan Abdul Hamid II with "Virginia's pay-as-you-go Sultan," Senator Harry Byrd. Whereas the original Young Turks rebelled against a leader who turned over the revenues of Turkey to a foreign bondholders' committee, the 1950s-era Young Turks rebelled against a U.S. senator who was notorious for keeping such a tight grip on spending that the state's infrastructure was literally crumbling. In other words, the two reform movements shared little more than youth.

"There is nothing radical about the Young Turks," Muse concluded. "They are liberals only in the Virginia sense. They are to the left of Abdul Hamid."

The success the Young Turks had in finally pumping some money into the badly neglected educational system in Virginia would end up being their swan song. Walter Page left the House to take a job as a judge in Norfolk. Armistead Boothe and Stuart Carter left the House to move across the hall to the Senate, where the median age was significantly higher than in the House. Although they could brag about increased funding for schools, they were unable to deliver on repealing the poll tax. If they had, perhaps the Byrd Machine might have been saved from the cataclysm to come.

Chapter 9

MASSIVE RESISTANCE

The Machine Combats Segregation with Systemic Racism

The Byrd Machine was not ready for *Brown v. Board*. The 1954 Supreme Court decision hit the organization like a sneak attack, exposing a fatal inability to adapt and an unwillingness to compromise. The decision to shut down public schools instead of desegregate tore the Byrd Machine apart and set the stage for its demise.

It all started in Farmville. That's where students organized a strike protesting poor conditions at Moton High School, a fire hazard with bad heating and a leaky roof. Water fountains were few and far between, and the auditorium was so small that any kind of assembly was overcrowded and stifling. The Prince Edward County school system promised to build a new school in 1946, but five years dragged on without any action or funding. Finally, the students had enough, and they organized a walkout.

Just before noon on a Monday morning in April 1951, more than 450 students walked out of the school. They picketed and carried signs that read, "We want a new school or none at all," "We are tied of tar-paper shacks" and "Down with tar-paper shacks." Members of the student council began canvassing the white citizens of Farmville about segregation, asking them if they really wanted to continue having separate and unequal school facilities. The parent-teacher association called an emergency meeting, where the NAACP argued that a new Black high school would solve nothing.

"If it were built brick for brick, cement for cement, the prestige could not equal that of a white school because of discrimination," declared Lester Banks, executive director of Virginia's NAACP chapter.[152]

The Supreme Court outlawed segregated schools in 1954 with its *Brown v. Board* decision. *Library of Congress.*

Members of the all-white school board were invited to that meeting, but none of them attended. The snub was an indication that they didn't particularly care about the concerns of the students, and the students vowed to continue the strike indefinitely until they were given a date when construction would begin for a new school. They organized a parade through the streets of downtown Farmville.

"We don't care if it takes two years," one student told the Associated Press. "We plan to stay out until we get some concrete information on the new school."[153]

The strike went on for two weeks, a time when school officials threatened disciplinary action against students they considered to be playing hooky. The students may not have been getting a formal education during that time, but they were certainly getting a crash course in constitutional law. By the time they returned to school, they had legal representation from the Richmond-based firm Hill, Martin and Robinson. The lawyers sent a petition to the Prince Edward County School Board members demanding they cease and desist segregating schools, warning that they were prepared to file a federal lawsuit if they didn't get a satisfactory answer.

The school board voted to reject the petition and retained the services of the Richmond-based law firm Hunton, Williams, Anderson, Gay and Moore. The students responded by filing a lawsuit in federal court asking that the court restrain Prince William schools from enforcing the provision of the state constitution requiring segregated schools. On May 22, 1951, one hundred students and their parents filed a twenty-two-page complaint arguing they were suffering "irreparable injury and are threatened with irreparable injury in the future."

Tar paper covers the windows at Moton High School in Farmville, where students led a revolt that led to school desegregation. *From the* Richmond Times-Dispatch.

A statue of Barbara Johns now graces Capitol Square in Richmond. *Michael Lee Pope.*

One of the most prominent students leading the charge was Barbara Johns, the niece of a legendary minister who worked with Martin Luther King Jr. at Dexter Street Baptist Church. The connection with King may have provided star power to the Johns family, but it didn't give them top billing in the legal case. The lawsuit was styled *Davis et al. v. County Board of Prince William County* because Dorothy Davis was the first student listed in the complaint, a ninth-grade student who was the daughter of a local farmer.

On the other side of the issue were lawyers representing the school board, who argued that Black schools in Prince Edward were just as good as white schools. Considering Virginia's reputation for funding education, it wasn't saying much. Joining them was Attorney General Lindsay Almond, who said that the inherent morality in Virginia's education program eliminated discrimination.

A trial was scheduled for February 1952 at the federal courthouse in Richmond, a building now known as the Lewis Powell United States Courthouse. A three-judge panel was assembled for the trial that included some of the most prominent names in Virginia legal circles: Albert Bryan of Alexandria, Sterling Hutcheson of Richmond and Armistead Dobie of Norfolk. It was clear to everyone involved that the case had an outsized influence.

The trial for the Farmville case happened at the federal courthouse in Richmond, now known as the Lewis Powell United States Courthouse. *Library of Virginia.*

"I think you can say it is of national or even international importance," declared Judge Dobie.[154]

Plaintiffs introduced 101 exhibits, including pictures comparing white facilities to Black schools and photostatic copies of school records and statistical compilations. At the center of their legal case was a comparison between Moton High School for Black students and Farmville High School for white students, a contrast that could not have possibly been clearer. Even advocates for segregation were forced to admit that conditions were not equal. Nevertheless, they marshaled budget numbers to show that they supposedly made investments that were comparable. That was enough for the three-judge panel, which ruled in favor of separate-but-equal schools.

Attorney General Lindsay Almond said that Virginia pursued a policy of "equalization of facilities." *Library of Congress.*

"Virginia recognizes and has progressively pursued a policy of equalization of facilities," said Attorney General Almond after the ruling was announced in March. "If there is to be an appeal, we'll meet it at the proper place at the proper time."[155]

The proper place was the U.S. Supreme Court. The proper time was 1954, when the Supreme Court ruled in *Brown v. Board of Education of Topeka*. The landmark ruling combined five cases across the country, including *Davis v. County School Board of Prince Edward County*. On May 17, 1954, the Supreme Court issued a unanimous ruling in the case, overturning the three-judge panel in Virginia and declaring segregated schools unconstitutional.

"It was a black Monday for Senator Byrd," wrote Byrd biographer Alden Hatch. "Friends who were with him say that he was literally stunned by the decision of the court."[156]

Byrd employed Black men in his orchards, and he worked with them and ate with them. He paid the same wages to white workers that he paid to Black workers, and he comforted their families in moments of sorrow. He paid their medical bills when they got sick, and he seems to have genuinely believed in equal justice before the law. But he did not believe Blacks were his equals.

Above: The landmark *Brown v. Board* decision combined five cases across the country, including *Davis v. County School Board of Prince Edward County*. *Library of Congress.*

Opposite: Governor Thomas Stanley was a former Speaker of the House who served three terms in Congress before becoming governor. *Library of Virginia.*

"There is no denying that Byrd was a racist in the modern sense of the word," concluded Hatch.[157]

A year after *Brown v. Board*, the court followed up with a vague ruling outlining how the decision should be implemented. The decision, now known as *Brown II*, ordered that the dismantling of separate schools for Black and white students should happen "with all deliberate speed." What the heck did that mean? Nobody really knew.

"Judges and lawyers might spend the rest of the 20th century arguing about what the court meant," responded Congressman Richard Harding Poff, a Republican from Radford. "It looks as if the Supreme Court wants the states to cut the puppy's tail off a little bit at a time so it won't hurt so much."[158]

The governor who happened to be sitting in the Executive Mansion when all this happened was Thomas Stanley of Henry County, a former Speaker of the House of Delegates who served three terms in Congress before stepping down to run for governor. He was the Byrd Machine candidate to take over after Bill Tuck. Although he had not campaigned on segregation, the issue was about to hijack his term of governor.

"I shall call together as quickly as practicable representatives of both state and local governments to consider the matter and work toward a plan which will be acceptable to our citizens and in keeping with the edit of the court," the governor said in a written statement after the decision. "Views of leaders of both races will be invited in the course of these studies."[159]

Stanley did not stand by that promise. In fact, he totally abandoned it at the suggestion of state Senator Garland Gray from Waverly. Gray was a staunch Southside segregationist who began his political career on the Sussex County School Board in 1925. He was elected to the Senate in 1941, and by 1954 he was chairman of the Senate Democratic Caucus. He served as campaign treasurer for Stanley's campaign for governor, so the senator also had significant influence at the Executive Mansion. Gray suggested the commission should be all lawmakers—nobody else. Stanley agreed and appointed thirty-four white men.

"I shall use every legal means at my command to preserve segregated public schools in Virginia," explained Governor Stanley.[160]

Senator Garland Gray of Waverly was a staunch Southside segregationist who led the commission charged with responding to *Brown v. Board*. *Library of Virginia*.

The General Assembly had no Black lawmakers, so the plan to restrict membership to elected officials was a surefire way to eliminate Blacks from consideration. The official name of the group was the State Commission on Public Education, but nobody called it that. Everyone called it the Gray Commission because the governor not only took Gray's advice about limiting the membership to lawmakers but also appointed the senator from Waverly as chairman. It had nineteen delegates and thirteen senators—all white, mostly from south of the James River. Although the commission was technically bipartisan, it had only two Republicans.

"Apart from the Republicans, virtually all the appointees are generally regular member of the dominant, conservative state Democratic organization," the *Times-Dispatch* reported.[161]

The commission included a few Young Turks, who had given the machine a hard time earlier that year. But it was dominated by organization men, including two future Byrd Machine governors: Albertis Harrison and Mills Godwin, who were both in the Senate at the time. One of the chief orders of business for the commission was scheduling a public hearing. At first, the venue was going to be the House chamber at the Capitol. But so many people expressed an interest in speaking that they had to move it to the grand Mosque Theater in Richmond, a building now known as the Altria Theater. That marathon hearing was attended by more than two thousand people

The Mosque Theater in Richmond was the scene of a marathon public hearing where people expressed a variety of views on how the schools should handle desegregation. *Library of Virginia.*

and featured more than one hundred speakers, adjourned after fourteen hours shortly before midnight on November 16, 1954.

Most of the white speakers urged the commission to find some way to keep segregation. That was the overwhelming sentiment of the day, as white speaker after white speaker worried that segregation would harm both races. Speakers included elected officials from Richmond, Mecklenburg, Sussex, Halifax, Buckingham, Dinwiddie and Lunenburg. Several speakers argued for avoiding integration by creating a system of three sets of schools, one white, one Black and another integrated. Several speakers said that they'd rather have no public schools at all than integrated schools. Ultimately, there was a lot of suspicion of the advocates for equality.

"The public schools should not be turned over to professional agitators," said William Story, superintendent of South Norfolk schools. "A small, garrulous minority of both races is trying to force a complete amalgamation of races."[162]

All the Black speakers argued for integration, and several white speakers joined them in pushing for desegregation. Although many whites made the case that segregation benefited Blacks, none of the African American speakers shared that view. Many of the speakers who advocated for carrying out the Supreme Court's mandate were from the religious community, people who viewed the conversation as a righteous struggle. One of the highlights of the day was a speech from Oliver Hill, one of the lawyers

Civil rights attorney Oliver Hill argues in favor of desegregation to members of the General Assembly, including Senator Albertis Harrison (*at the lower left*). *From the Richmond Times-Dispatch.*

representing the Prince Edward students in the legal case that led to the Supreme Court decision.

"The proponents of desegregation look at life from the present into the future while the proponents of segregation look at life from the present into the past," said Hill. "Gentlemen, face the dawn and not the setting sun. A new day is being born."[163]

The marathon public hearing at the Mosque was the only hint at transparency. Every other gathering of the Gray Commission happened behind closed doors, secret meetings that went on for fourteen months. Even as the commission was preparing a draft of the report, any hint at what might be in it was a closely guarded secret. Finally, in November 1955, a year after the Mosque public hearing, Gray was finally ready to unveil the recommendations of his commission. The nineteen-page report was essentially a blueprint for sidestepping integration, providing public education funding to private schools and arming local governments with broad powers to assign pupils anywhere they wanted. Ostensibly, race was not supposed to be a factor in moving students around, but the reason for the pupil assignment plan was to sidestep the Supreme Court's order. The *Richmond Times-Dispatch* praised the plan for its flexibility.

"If a county or city wishes to experiment with an arrangement whereby all boys of both races are sent to one school and all girls to another, it can do so," proclaimed the editorial board. "If it wants to try to set up a system under which there will per one school for whites, one for Negroes and a third for those who desire integration, it can do that too."[164]

The bottom line for the Gray Commission is that no child should be required to attend an integrated school. The only race mixing would be done by school divisions that wanted to integrate, an option that was wildly unpopular at the time. The so-called pupil assignment plan could be done under the guise of health, aptitude or availability of transportation. But everyone knew that it was designed to maintain segregation. The tuition grants were really a way to undermine the idea of public education, a concept that was clearly headed in the direction of mixing white children with Black children.

"The recommendations of the commission are legally indefensible, morally wrong and economically unsound," said NAACP President E.B. Henderson of Falls Church.[165]

Two members of the commission—Senator Mills Godwin of Suffolk and Delegate Samuel Pope of Southampton—feared that the report did not go far enough. They signed on to the report, but they believed it needed "further safeguards." Pope said he "led the fight all the way through this thing," adding that he worried the final version of the report acknowledged the possibility that some localities might integrate their schools. He and Godwin were concerned that the Gray Commission report might end up being interpreted as a modified integration plan.

Harry Byrd issued a one-thousand-word statement from Winchester endorsing the tuition grants while carefully avoiding any discussion of the local option, foreshadowing his approach in the future. Although he was agreeing with the recommendations of the Gray Commission, he was also in no hurry to take action. In fact, he specifically avoided any action that would make any changes to the upcoming school term in September 1956.

"I feel that the emphasis should be on deliberate rather than speed," said Byrd. "The road ahead of us will be long and rocky."[166]

The road ahead was certainly long and rocky for anyone trying to oppose the Byrd Machine. Opposition to the plan outlined in the Gray Commission was poorly financed and scattered, although a new group was created specifically to work against tuition grants. Known as the Society for the Preservation of Public Schools, it was formed by Armistead Boothe, who was now a senator representing Alexandria. He liked the idea of pupil placement but thought that tuition grants were unconstitutional and "an inducement to close the public schools" in some areas.

"The assignment plan will serve to retain segregation in Virginia schools for as long as the social order in the various parts of Virginia demands it," Boothe said during a radio debate. "Let's try the assignment plan first. It will preserve out Southern traditions within the law."[167]

Opponents of segregation seized on a long-forgotten bit of history to make sure Black students were prevented from walking into white schools: interposition, the idea that Virginia had authority to interpose itself to thwart federal overreach. The concept dated back to 1789, when the General Assembly passed a resolution of interposition refusing to obey the Alien and Sedition Laws. A series of editorials in the *Richmond News Leader* by editor James Jackson Kilpatrick outlined how the moribund idea could be revived to prevent integration. The idea was wildly popular in the General Assembly, which approved an interposition resolution ninety to five in the House and thirty-six to two in the Senate.

"Let no man in the Senate or elsewhere read into this resolution a nullification," said Senator Albertis Harrison of Lawrenceville, a future governor. "It points out usurpation and does it in a dignified and restrained manner."[168]

"This is nothing but double talk," declared Delegate Robert Whitehead of Nelson County. "If it is not your intention to nullify then why is this resolution cluttered with the offspring of nullification?"[169]

A few days later, the attorney general declared that the interposition resolution was not a legislative enactment and did not have the force of law. Perhaps even more significantly, it could not be asserted as a defense in court. But that was never the point anyway. The resolution was an attempt to harden Virginia's resistance to segregation, setting the stage for a handful of other southern states to follow suit. The hysteria around interposition changed the dynamic of the debate over integration, and the machine was now pushing to ditch the idea and replace the Gray Plan with a new plan: massive resistance.

"If we can organize the southern states for massive resistance to this order I think that in time the rest of the country will realize that racial integration is not going to be accepted in the South," declared Senator Byrd on February 25, 1956. "In interposition, the South has a perfectly legal means of appeal from the Supreme Court's order."[170]

A few months earlier, Governor Stanley gave a wholehearted endorsement to the Gray Commission's plan. Now the tide had turned, and the machine turned against the idea of a local option. Speaker Blackburn Moore introduced a resolution providing that lawmakers would do nothing in preparation for the upcoming school year in 1956, formally turning his back on the idea that local school divisions would have the option of integrating. Instead, the machine moved all its pieces on the chessboard toward massive resistance.

"The Supreme Court of the United States reversed itself," noted Delegate Robert Whitehead. "Next Governor Stanley reversed himself. Now the Gray Commission has reversed itself. This leaves the situation in a state of profound confusion."[171]

The Gray Commission plan was replaced by what became known as the Stanley Plan, the Byrd Machine's strategy for using the executive authority of the governor's office to carry out massive resistance. Governor Stanley summoned lawmakers to Richmond for yet another special session. This would be the third time the General Assembly would meet in ten months. The Stanley Plan included thirteen bills aimed at closing or cutting off state funding for schools that tried to integrate.

"There can be no compromise because any integration would be fatal," said Senator James Hagood, chairman of the Senate Finance Committee. "A state policy for Virginia must be set by this General Assembly. It is needed as a deterrent to any locality in Virginia which has, or will, indicate a willingness to integrate under an assignment law."[172]

When Stanley left office, he was quite proud of the fact that no Black students had entered a white school during his administration. Senator Byrd apparently wanted him to be succeeded by Garland Gray, who helped navigate the treacherous waters of responding to *Brown v. Board*. But Gray dropped out of the race when longtime Attorney General Lindsay Almond announced his candidacy. In the fall of 1957, Almond faced a challenge from Republican Ted Dalton, who gave Stanley a run for his money four years earlier. The chief issue of the election was massive resistance.

Lindsay Almond had been part of the Byrd Machine since the 1920s. He served in Congress and as Virginia's attorney general before becoming governor. *Library of Congress.*

"My plan is to resist at every step by attempting to meet as effectively as possible every situation which may confront us in the days ahead," he said on the campaign trail. "Virginia's defense has been and will continue to be a defense in depth. Under this defense no schools have closed and no integration has taken place."[173]

A native of Charlottesville, Almond was the son of a Southern Railway locomotive engineer who retired to the family farm in Orange County after a head-on collision. The rolling hills of the 250-acre property were near the village of Locust Grove on the Chancellorsville battlefield, where Confederate General Stonewall Jackson was accidentally killed by his own men. As a young man, Almond worked in a sawmill, sowed wheat and milked cows to earn enough to go to the University of Virginia. In 1925, he joined Harry Byrd's campaign for governor and became part of the machine. When Byrd was elected governor, Almond was rewarded with a spot on the hustings court in Roanoke, appointing courthouse officials who oversaw most local expenditures.

Almond was elected to Congress in 1946, but he didn't stay there long. In February 1948, Virginia Attorney General Harvey Apperson unexpectedly died. Almond gave up his $15,000 House salary to head to Richmond and take the $10,000 job of attorney general. It may have paid less, but it set him up to be in line for the Executive Mansion—in theory anyway.

Almond stumbled a bit by writing a letter in favor of President Truman's appointment of Martin Hutchinson to the Federal Trade Commission. Hutchinson was Virginia's leading anti-Byrd Democrat, and the letter of support of Hutchinson was a misstep that put him in the doghouse for years.

Almond's performance in the U.S. Supreme Court probably should have been enough to land him the Byrd Machine's nod for governor in 1953. But the personal slight of supporting Hutchinson caused Byrd to push him aside, choosing the lackluster Congressman Stanley instead. Now that Almond was finally taking office, the limits of Virginia's resolve were about to be tested. He was in an awkward position of being an excellent lawyer defending a weak argument.

"Governor Lindsay Almond remains much too good a lawyer to believe that Virginia's massive resistance laws will hold water in court," noted *Time* magazine in May 1948. "But Politician Almond is in much too deep to back out, and as the local figure in enforcing massive resistance, he has recently seen his position deteriorate almost daily."[174]

After Almond was safely installed in the Executive Mansion, Senator Byrd announced that he would not be running for a fifth term in 1958. After more than three decades in public service, he decided that he wanted to return home to Rosemont and take care of his ailing wife. It's impossible to overestimate the reaction to the news, which hit the world of Virginia politics like an atom bomb. The House and Senate approved resolutions begging him to reconsider, and party leaders worried that the vacancy created would launch a civil war between former Governors Bill Tuck and John Battle. Ultimately, Byrd decided to run again one last time, and he was reelected with 69 percent of the vote.

"I am keenly aware of my errors in judgment in this long period of holding office," he said after securing his last political victory. "But I can say to you with all my sincerity that I have done my very best to be faithful to Virginia and worthy of her great traditions."[175]

The fight over massive resistance was already edging the machine toward a breaking point, and now was no time to back down as the 1958–59 school year was about to begin. The machine would need all the massive resistance Byrd could muster to resist the will of the Supreme Court. It was a fight that began in Front Royal, where the courts ordered Warren County High School to integrate. Even though Governor Almond never really bought into the school-closing laws, he was the executive tasked with carrying out the plan.

C45 Lane High School, Charlottesville, Va.

81411

Lane High School in Charlottesville was one of the schools to close during massive resistance. *Library of Virginia.*

"I am willing to continue the fight to the last ditch and then dig another ditch," explained Almond. "We might have to take it between the eyes."[176]

Next came two schools in Charlottesville, Lane High School and Venable Elementary School. Many of those students ended up in private schools with makeshift quarters. The situation was more extreme in Norfolk, where thousands of junior high students and senior high students found themselves without any kind of classroom. As school after school closed, a sense of resentment grew among white elites that their schools were being ruined. Senator Edward Willey of Richmond suggested that Black schools be closed as a matter of revenge.

"It's a case of equality," said Willey. "If we are going to operate private schools in communities for whites, then we should operate private schools for Negro children."[177]

The Norfolk City Council voted to end all public education beyond the sixth grade in anticipation of the courts intervening, which is exactly what happened in January 1959. The Supreme Court of Virginia outlawed school closings with a vote of five to two, declaring that the state must support public schools for pupils of both races "however unfortunate that situation may be." Then a three-judge panel in Norfolk ruled that the new law calling for school closings violated the Fourteenth Amendment. The one-two punch from the courts seemed to apply massive resistance to massive resistance.

"It's like a baseball game," said Senator William Stone of Martinsville. "It goes to nine innings, and the nine innings aren't up yet."[178]

The game was clearly not over yet for the governor, who went on live radio and television to deliver a blistering speech vowing to continue the fight. Almond later came to regret it, referring to it as "that damn speech." Yet his sense of outrage seemed to meet the moment for white Virginians who wanted their governor to push as hard as possible to keep Black children away from their all-white public schools. The fifteen-minute speech left no doubt that Almond would continue unyielding resistance to race mixing in Virginia's public schools.

"To those who defend or close their eyes to the livid stench of sadism, sex, immorality and juvenile pregnancy infesting the mixed schools of the District of Columbia and elsewhere," the governor explained, "let me make it abundantly clear for the record now and hereafter, as governor of this state, I will not yield to that which I know to be wrong and will destroy every rational semblance of education for thousands of children in Virginia."

Almond castigated those of "faint heart," declaring war against "false prophets" who sought "token integration." He cast himself as the defender of "customs, morals and tradition," vowing to oppose the "new moral code prepared by nine men in Washington." He pledged to oppose anyone who wanted to "blend and amalgamate the white and Negro race and destroy the integrity of both races." Ultimately, he said, he would stand at the schoolhouse door and protect it against "those who would destroy our way of life because of their pretend concern over what Soviet Russia may think of us."

"No price is too high to pay; no burden too heavy to bear," he concluded, "no consequence too grave to endure in defense of the right and duty of this commonwealth to protect the people of Virginia in the proper enjoyment of their right and obligation to mold the character and promote the welfare of their children through the exercise of their voice and judgement in their education and development."[179]

Almond would later admit that he was tired and distraught and not thinking clearly when he gave the speech, which would haunt him the rest of his life. His intention was to communicate to Virginians that he didn't agree with the court's opinions and that he would do everything in his power to resist them. Unfortunately, though, he ended up giving the impression that he knew more than he was letting on. Many people assumed that he wouldn't be saying these things unless he had a plan to prevent integration when, in fact, he did not. Eight days later, he appeared before a joint session of the General Assembly and admitted that all he could do was minimize racial mixing in the schools.

"No fair-minded person would be so unreasonable as to seek to hold me responsible for failure to exercise powers which that state is powerless to bestow," said Almond. "I have repeatedly stated that I did not possess the power and knew of none that could be evolved that would enable Virginia to overthrow or negate the overriding power of the federal government."[180]

Almond's plan was to repeal the compulsory-education law and press forward with a different type of tuition grant. That would be paired with stronger laws against violence. All of that would be accompanied by the tried-and-true action of any Virginia pol in a no-win scenario: appoint a commission to study the issue and write a report. Compared to the rip-snorting tone of his defiant radio and television speech, the sober address to the General Assembly left many of the most virulent segregationists beside themselves with disappointment.

"The massive resisters were thunderstruck," noted longtime *Times-Dispatch* editor Virginius Dabney. "Almond was sneeringly referred to by some of them thereafter as Benedict Almond."[181]

The era of massive resistance ended at 8:45 a.m. on February 2, 1959, when four Black students entered Stratford Junior High in the Cherrydale neighborhood of Arlington. Fifteen minutes later, seventeen Black students enrolled in six Norfolk secondary schools. Tensions were high, and both schools had a heavy police presence. But there were no pickets, no mobs and no violence. Unlike other southern states where integration had become an ugly spectacle, the scene in Arlington and Norfolk was relatively calm and peaceful.

"In the long view of history, it may be yet shown that Virginia's frustrating and negative experience with massive resistance was necessary to produce acceptance of desegregation as preferable to closed schools," noted a *Washington Post* editorial. "It may be, indeed, that Governor Almond himself understood this, and that his forensics of two weeks ago at the expense of the Washington schools were designed to facilitate the inevitable adjustment by showing Southside Virginia that he had done his utmost legally to preserve segregation."[182]

When the commission, headed by Senator Mosby Perrow of Lynchburg, finally issued its report, the chief recommendation was for a local option, or "freedom of choice." Under the proposal, local school boards would be required to excuse any child from attending a school if parents signed an affidavit declaring they "conscientiously object." But getting that through

The era of massive resistance came to an end in 1959 when four Black students entered Stratford Junior High School in the Cherrydale neighborhood of Arlington. *Library of Congress.*

a Senate Education Committee dominated by an old guard hell-bent on massive resistance would take some finagling. It would ultimately be accomplished by a legislative sleight of hand, bypassing the committee where it would have surely failed to report. Instead, senators voted twenty to nineteen to resolve the Senate into a Committee of the Whole. It was a "slap in the face to everyone on the Education Committee," declared Senator Harold Purcell of Louisa.[183]

The House of Delegates added so many amendments to the Almond-Perrow school program that the massive resistance bloc had any number of escape hatches. So, after the drama over the parliamentary votes on resolving the Senate into a Committee on the Whole were out of the way, opposition to the merits of the plan withered away. The final vote was thirty to six, sending the bill to Almond's desk so he could essentially sign the death certificate of massive resistance.

"I lived in hell," Almond later remarked about the era of massive resistance.[184]

His "freedom of choice" legislation broke the back of the segregationists. The governor could have gone "the last mile" and made a show of being arrested and going to jail. But his resistance was just not that massive, certainly not enough for the head of the Byrd Machine. Harry Byrd held a grudge, and the two never spoke again. Years later, when President John Kennedy appointed Almond to the U.S. Court of Customs and Patent Appeals, Byrd held up the appointment for more than fourteen months as a matter of revenge. Nevertheless, Almond said he would choose Byrd as the greatest Virginian in public life.

"Mr. Byrd never forgave me, but I'm not going to let that affect my choice," Almond said in 1967. "Yes, I suppose that mine may be a charitable view when you consider his treatment of me in the last years of his life."[185]

Chapter 10

BEGINNING OF THE END

The 1965 Election Turned Out to Be a Swan Song for the Organization

After the disaster of massive resistance, the Byrd Machine entered a state of decline. Virginia's suburbs were growing fast, and the old pay-as-you-go system of financing capital projects was increasingly seen as anachronistic and counterproductive. The 1965 election for governor offers an important window into how the death throes of the organization translated on the campaign trail, essentially a swan song for the machine. Byrd was able to get his man in the Executive Mansion, but Mills Godwin would be the last candidate to get the nod. And the whole operation would flame out in the next election.

The setting for the election of Godwin was, of course, the 1964 election in which Lyndon Johnson won Virginia and the election. It was the first time Democrats won Virginia since 1948, which is a significant period of time for the commonwealth to be a reliably Republican state. But 1964 offered some significant differences from previous elections. Although Johnson was not elected president in 1960, the assassination of John Kennedy put him in the White House, so he was running for reelection.

Perhaps more significant was the demise of the poll tax, which was the secret to the Byrd Machine success in election after election. Depressing the turnout allowed the organization to maximize its influence with a limited number of voters. The institutionalized racism, of course, was aimed at keeping Black people from exercising the franchise. And it worked for decades. That all came crashing down after the ratification of the Twenty-Fourth Amendment.

Right: The election of Mills Godwin as governor in 1965 was the death knell for the Byrd Machine. Soon enough, Republicans would take the Executive Mansion, and the machine would be inextricably broken. *Library of Virginia.*

Below: When Lyndon Johnson won Virginia in 1964, it was the first time Democrats won the Commonwealth since 1948. *Library of Congress.*

Opposite: The Lady Bird Special made stops across the South, where the first lady campaigned for the Democratic ticket. *Library of Congress.*

"Future historians looking back at 1964 may well seize upon the demise of the poll tax in federal elections, and the organization's failure to find a voter-control substitute, as the most significant political development of the year in Virginia," observed journalist James Latimer in the *Richmond Times-Dispatch.*[186]

Godwin was hoping to make the time-honored leap from lieutenant governor to governor, but he had to figure out how to do so in an environment with shifting tectonic plates. Virginia was becoming more centrist and perhaps even more progressive. Power was shifting from the small cities and towns of rural Virginia to urban areas, and so Godwin sought to refashion his image from being a supporter of massive resistance to an advocate for industrial development and expanded services. Although the Byrd Machine's golden silence on Democratic presidential candidates had been the tradition, Godwin broke the spell and aligned himself with Johnson despite his big-government, big-spending Great Society agenda.

"For three years as lieutenant governor, he had traveled throughout the state, and he had his finger on the pulse of the party," observed historian Frank Atkinson. "The Democratic Party in Virginia was moving toward the center, pressures for more progressive policies were mounting, and patience with the part-time party loyalty of some of the Byrd leaders was wearing thin."[187]

And so when the Johnson campaign asked Godwin to board the "Lady Bird Special," it was an offer that was too good to refuse. Although it may have been a move that was viewed with suspicion among lieutenants of the Byrd Machine, boarding the campaign train was a recommendation of Sydney Kellam, one of Byrd's closest allies who was now manager for the Johnson campaign in Virginia.

President Johnson rode the train to Union Station in Alexandria, where Lieutenant Governor Godwin introduced him. As a strategic move, it was a way for Godwin to divorce himself from the inherent racism of massive resistance. He could use the president and his Great Society agenda as a way to springboard a new image for himself, although he understood the risk associated with breaking the golden silence. Many of Virginia's hardcore segregationists hated Johnson and his support for civil rights, considering him a traitor to the Lost Cause.

Godwin's chief competition came from the scion of the machine, Harry Byrd Jr. But after discussing the matter with his father, the son decided that it would be inappropriate for two Byrds to be on the ticket that year. The senior Byrd was once again running for reelection to his final term in the Senate. And having his namesake seeking to hold the position his father once held seemed dangerously close to malicious nepotism. Ultimately, the calculus was that two machine candidates battling for supremacy would open the door to an anti-machine candidate to win the election—perhaps someone like Congressman Pat Jennings.

The official word was that the younger Byrd had business and personal reasons to avoid the race, specifically mentioning a desire to spend more time with his recently widowed father. Whatever the reason, Byrd's announcement that he would not be a candidate for governor removed the last significant obstacle to Godwin receiving the nod. The lieutenant governor announced his candidacy for governor in January 1965 emphasizing education as the key issue in the race.

"Without rapid educational expansion now, Virginia simply will not share fully in the economic expansion of America," said Godwin in his announcement. "The needs of our public schools and institutions of higher education, as well as our technical schools, are many and acute, and we must give them highest priority."[188]

Godwin didn't say how he would pay for expanding public education, although he promised that he would find a new source of revenue if it was needed to balance the books. His support for Johnson reassured liberals about his party loyalty. And in private he was assuaging his critics that he had broadened his outlook since his days at the forefront of massive resistance.

"The primary reason for Godwin's new acceptability among liberals seems to be the decline of the race issue as a factor in state politics," wrote William Chapman in the *Washington Post*. "Judges, not politicians, settle the differences."[189]

Republicans didn't really pose much of a threat. In the last half century, the GOP was competitive in only one campaign for governor: the 1953 campaign of Ted Dalton, who ran as a progressive against the Byrd Machine candidate Thomas Stanley. In 1965, the Republican most interested in seeking the nomination was Linwood Holton of Roanoke. Unfortunately for ultraconservatives, Holton was more in

Linwood Holton was the Republican candidate for governor in 1965. He didn't win, but he set the stage for a successful campaign in 1969. *Virginia Historical Society.*

the mold of Dalton than the kind of candidate the right-wing Virginia Conservative Council wanted.

Dalton was a mentor to Holton, who ran twice unsuccessfully for the House of Delegates in the 1950s. In 1961, Dalton served as campaign manager to Republican Clyde Pearson during his race against Democrat Albertis Harrison. Four years later, Holton decided to throw his hat in the ring. As he later wrote in his memoir, *Opportunity Time*, it was a campaign that was intended more as an incremental movement rather than a triumphant victory.

"There was no chance for a Republican to win a Virginia gubernatorial race in 1965," Holton wrote.[190]

The idea was that he could seize the Republican nomination because nobody else wanted it after the debacle of the Barry Goldwater presidential campaign in 1964. Holton saw opportunity for vote sources in regular Republicans, African American voters, labor unions and moderates who were horrified by the blatant racism of massive resistance.

Even if he scored only 35 or 40 percent of the vote against Godwin in 1965, he would build name recognition and have the inside track against the Byrd Machine Democrat in 1969.

When the Conservative Council requested a meeting with Holton, the campaign had an important decision to make about perception. Even if Holton were to meet with the group and reject all of its demands, the meeting

Barry Goldwater's 1964 campaign had been such a disaster that many Virginia Republicans were reluctant to run for statewide office. *Library of Congress.*

itself would tarnish the GOP as an extension of the John Birch Society—a political advocacy organization dedicated to anti-communism and limited government. Conservative Council chairman John Carter of Danville was already upset with Godwin for campaigning with Johnson and being rejected by the Republicans opened the door to a development that threatened the Democrats' stranglehold on power.

Members of the Conservative Council created their own political party, the Conservative Party, and nominated their own slate of candidates. More than three hundred delegates met in Richmond at the Jefferson Hotel on July 10, 1965, to draft a platform and approve a slate of statewide candidates. At the top of the ticket was William Story, a segregationist member of the John Birch Society who was assistant superintendent of schools in Chesapeake. For lieutenant governor, the Conservative Party chose Reid Putney of Goochland, a forestry consultant and former Republican who left the party because he felt it was too liberal. Conservative Council chairman John Carter himself was nominated as the party's candidate for attorney general.

"This nation is going down the road to Marxism with such rapidity it is frightening," said Carter in a keynote speech.

Carter demonized Holton as "Rockefeller's fair-haired boy" who was backed by the "Rockefeller fortune." He attacked Godwin as "Lyndon's fair-

Conservative Party ticket in 1965. *From left to right*: Reid Putney, candidate for lieutenant governor; William Story, candidate for governor; and John Carter, candidate for attorney general. *From the* Richmond Times-Dispatch.

haired boy" backed by welfare payments funded by hardworking taxpayers. He said that neither candidate has "intestinal fortitude," and both offer nothing more than "pious platitudes." The platform called for investigating subversive influences, maintaining law and order in parts of Virginia "besieged by violence," eliminating "federal control" over Virginia schools and, of course, sticking to a pay-as-you-go spending philosophy.

"We cannot abandon this great hope," said Story, who told delegates that he would keep his day job with Chesapeake schools and campaign in his spare time. "We must struggle against this great evil."[191]

As if the election wasn't already crazy enough, there was also a Nazi running for governor. George Lincoln Rockwell, leader of the American Nazi Party, threw his hat into the ring and ran on a platform of white supremacy. The Nazi Party was located in Arlington, where it oversaw a national operation that distributed racist pamphlets across the country. Rockwell's strategy was racial polarization, and so on the campaign trail he threatened to arrest civil rights icon Martin Luther King Jr. and his aides if they returned to Virginia. When he announced his candidacy at a press conference in his suite at the Hotel John Marshall in Richmond, the Nazi chief said that he was already receiving financial support from Texas, California and Danville.

"If it depended only on Danville, we would be in now," Rockwell told reporters.[192]

George Lincoln Rockwell files his candidacy for governor. *From the* Richmond Times-Dispatch.

Rockwell must have suspected that he wasn't going to win, but he also knew that the publicity surrounding his campaign for governor would be a win-win proposition. His solution to the integration crisis was even more bold than the massive resistance. Rockwell wanted the curriculum to proclaim white people as superior and Black people as inferior—a move he assumed would prompt Black parents to withdraw their children from integrated schools. He was furious that the Conservative Party would divide his natural constituency.

"Realistically, Rockwell had no chance claiming Virginia's racists," wrote historian James Sweeney. "They might agree with him on his characterization of African-American leadership, but they were not Nazis. Rockwell's ranting posed no threat either to Story or Godwin."[193]

While the racists were divided between the Conservative Party and the Nazis, Godwin was putting together one of the most unlikely coalitions in Virginia political history. He was able to dispatch liberals like Armistead Boothe to campaign for him in Arlington and conservative congressman Bill Tuck to stump for him in Danville. The Godwin campaign was such

The 1965 Democratic ticket. *From left to right*: state Senator Fred Pollard, candidate for lieutenant governor; incumbent Attorney General Robert Button; and Lieutenant Governor Mills Godwin, candidate for governor. *From the* Richmond Times-Dispatch.

a big tent that it included Byrd Machine Democrats as well as anti-Byrd Machine Democrats—united in their opposition to Republicans, Nazis and the Conservative Council.

The last time a candidate managed to win against the Byrd Machine and the anti-machine was back in 1937, when James Price became governor even though he hadn't received the nod. Now, almost thirty years later, liberals like Henry Howell were endorsing Godwin—the machine candidate—for governor. Howell said that Godwin promised increased funding for higher education and mental institutions. Senator Byrd even issued a brief announcement of endorsement, although he waited until October to issue the written statement.

"In Virginia, we believe sound progress is built on fiscal conservatism, and we have the record to prove it," Byrd said in the statement from his Senate office. "Our public schools and institutions of higher learning provide splendid evidence that our Democratic leadership is meeting and discharging the demands of a growing population."[194]

Harry Byrd waited until October to endorse Mills Godwin for governor, issuing a brief written statement. *Special Collections, University of Virginia.*

On the campaign trail, Conservative Party candidate William Story had been saying that Godwin abandoned Byrd. But now, the senator weighing in on the campaign and breaking his silence was a kind of surprise for conservatives, some of whom were starting to question the fraying alliances of the machine. For now, they were able to keep the coalition together, although the tent may have been a bit bigger than expected.

Republican nominee for lieutenant governor Vince Callahan and Clarence Townes engage voters. *Virginia Commonwealth University.*

One of the many surprises in the campaign was labor's decision to embrace Godwin, a development that moved in a shockingly different direction from decades of conflict with the organization dating back to the VEPCO affair and the origins of the so-called "right to work" law outlawing union shops. Labor leaders liked Godwin supported President Johnson in 1964, and it's not like other candidates were fighting over the union vote. Godwin was the first and last machine candidate to win an endorsement from labor.

"We feel an atmosphere is developing in the Democratic Party, nationally and in Virginia, where management, labor and government can work more closely together for the benefit and the common good of all our society," according to the statement from the AFL-CIO.[195]

One of the new dynamics in Virginia politics at the time was the rising political power of Black voters. Because African Americans provided the margin of victory for Johnson in 1964, perspectives were shifting about what kind of influence they might have at the ballot box. The poll tax was still suppressing the vote, although the NAACP conducted drives to get Black

145

voters to pay their poll tax in time to be eligible to vote. Both sides were courting the Black vote.

"Some are for the Democrat, some are for the Republicans," one Black leader told the *Washington Post*, "and some are going fishing."[196]

The 1965 election also saw the reemergence of the Ku Klux Klan, which was spreading into Southside from North Carolina. As the fall campaign season ramped up, the KKK had more than thirty weekend rallies with hundreds in attendance. The parking lots at the rallies had an increasing number of automobiles with Conservative Party bumper stickers. They viewed the Democrats and the Republicans as working together as part of some Communist plot.

"We're for good old American patriotism," said Grand Dragon Marshall Kornegay.[197]

Godwin and Holton both made a public display of their rejection of the Klan, but Story refused to denounce the KKK. Racial tension created a backdrop for much of the campaign, including Holton's repeated claims that Godwin was a "school closer," invoking massive resistance. Issues took a backseat to personalities because the major party candidates agreed on increased expenditures on education and mental health.

"Mills Godwin is tweedle dum and Linwood Holton is tweedle dee," quipped Story. "Both should just be called twee."[198]

Although Story and the Conservative Party ticket skillfully avoided blatant racism during the campaign, they did everything they could to remind voters that Godwin campaigned for Johnson and his Great Society agenda. Rockwell was more direct in his appeal to white supremacy, although his campaign was so starved for attention it had to resort to stunts. During a rally in Fredericksburg, he brandished a rifle and suggested that guns protected white people during the recent riots in the Watts neighborhood of Los Angeles.

"All of you ought to own one of these," Rockwell said to a crowd of admirers.[199]

At the Virginia State Fair, Rockwell had a booth promoting his candidacy that featured a live monkey in a cage that had a sign proclaiming "Residence of Dr. Martin Luther Coon." The fair's operator obtained an injunction from the Henrico County Circuit Court ordering Rockwell and his associates to vacate the booth. Rockwell supporters would interrupt campaign events to ask Holton and Godwin why they were afraid to debate the Nazi leader. His stunts didn't seem to have much of an influence in the campaign, which was between the two major-party campaigns.

"While Godwin is reserved, rather formal and traditional in his approach to weeing Old Dominion voters, Holton is exuberant, folksy and sometimes impetuous in his happy warrior approach to campaigning," wrote Helen Dewar in the *Washington Post*. "Godwin is at his best before an audience of old friends. Holton's forte is person-to-person contact."[200]

In addition to his skills as a retail politician, Godwin also had several other significant advantages. His coalition included people who supported the machine and people who opposed the machine, as well as labor supporters and labor opponents alike. He also raised more than twice as much money, a financial edge that allowed him to advertise on television, radio and billboards. All the major newspapers endorsed the Democratic ticket.

"There are few issues on which the state Democratic leadership is vulnerable, given the certain prospect that the party leader's will recommend appropriation of huge additional sums at the approaching legislative session to care for Virginia's skyrocketing needs," the *Richmond Times Dispatch* editorial board wrote in its endorsement. "No widespread discontent exists, and certainly there have been no scandals in the state government to stir the voters."[201]

When Election Day finally arrived, Godwin won as expected although with a margin of victory that was shockingly low. The Democrat secured only 48 percent of the vote, which meant it was the first ticket in modern history to win with less than a majority of voters. Perhaps the real significance of the election was that it served as a transition from one era to another.

The election of Mills Godwin as governor in 1965 marked the last time the Byrd Machine was able to exercise power by giving a candidate "the nod" and having him win election for governor. Soon enough, the young Republicans would be able to win statewide, and liberal Democrats would split with the remnants of the ailing old machine.

Black voters in Richmond, Norfolk and Petersburg gave Godwin the edge he needed to win, which is perhaps ironic considering his role in massive resistance. The Conservative Party did a little better than expected, but the division between Story and the major-party candidates showed that ultra-conservatism didn't really have a home in mainstream politics. In the end, Godwin won by putting together a coalition that included conservatives, liberals, moderates, union supporters, union opponents and African Americans.

"Were ever such bedfellows united in one boarding house?" asked *Richmond News Leader* editor James Jackson Kilpatrick.[202]

Holton did not get elected, at least not this time. But he achieved his goal of increasing his name recognition and setting himself up for a future statewide campaign. He described Godwin's shaky coalition as a "house of cards," a keen observation considering that the Byrd Machine was about to fall apart.

THE MACHINE FALLS APART

D etermining the end of the Byrd Machine is somewhat of a challenge, and there are probably many different answers to the question. One way to pinpoint the moment might be the death of Harry Byrd in October 1966. Another contender is the slow but steady erosion of conservative Democrats to the Republican Party, a trend that would move Mills Godwin and Harry Byrd Jr. to the Grand Old Party. But perhaps the most dramatic moment of reckoning for the rusty old organization was when it lost the Executive Mansion.

The 1969 election was a watershed moment in Virginia politics. The Democrats were backing William Battle for governor. He got the nod from what was left of the machine, which was now a zombie of sorts—acting out of longstanding habits and perpetual motion. Battle was a Charlottesville lawyer and the son of former Governor John Battle. The senior Battle was governor during the peak of Byrd Machine power, so the gold-plated name surely had a powerful influence across the conservative rural areas that the machine had been cultivating for so many decades.

But Virginia was shifting. More people were moving to urban areas, increasing demand for liberal policies. And in 1966, the Supreme Court issued a ruling that outlawed the use of the poll tax for state elections. That meant Black voters could vote in much greater numbers and even determine the outcome of an election. This was the environment in which Republican Linwood Holton, making his second campaign for governor, would triumph over the machine, ending its long streak of selecting governors. The Godwin

Above: The official portrait of Governor Linwood Holton hangs in the third floor of the Capitol. *Library of Virginia.*

Opposite: Perhaps the most lasting legacy of the Byrd Machine is Virginia's conservative approach to government spending. *Library of Congress.*

coalition had evaporated, and voters elected the first Republican governor of the twentieth century.

"Holton tied his candidacy firmly to President Nixon and pitched his campaign to the cry of 'it's time for change' after 84 years of Democratic gubernatorial regimes," wrote James Latimer in the *Richmond Times Dispatch*. "Defections from the conservative and liberal fringes of what once was considered Virginia's normal Democratic majority apparently supplied Holton's margin of victory."[203]

People who benefited from the machine all those years must have hoped for some kind of comeback, a way to make Virginia great again. When Harry Byrd Sr. announced his retirement from the Senate in November 1965, Governor Albertis Harrison appointed Harry Byrd Jr. to fill the seat. The dying machine would still have a Byrd in the U.S. Senate. But the junior Byrd would never have the same kind of machine his father once operated.

The influence of the Byrd Machine has a strong hold on the imagination of Virginians. Many people believe the Byrd Machine to be the root of all evil in Virginia politics, blaming it for everything from the poll tax and the short ballot to voter apathy and institutional rot. In some ways this is understandable. The Byrd Machine certainly depended on the poll tax to

Harry Byrd Jr. and President Lyndon Johnson. *Library of Congress.*

suppress the vote so its members could stay in power, so it was central to the organization. But the Byrd Machine inherited the poll tax from the Martin Machine.

The short ballot is a different story. Clearly, Byrd was the mastermind of Virginia's peculiar system of having so few people on the ballot and so many people operating in the smoke-filled back rooms of Richmond. Even now, more than fifty years after the machine fell apart, the Byrd Machine organization of government is still with us. It's a system that puts outsized influence into the hands of the governor, who gets to appoint many officials who would be elected in other states.

These days, the legacy of the Byrd Machine is thoroughly tied to massive resistance. The powers that be placed all their chips on a bet they lost. And they lost spectacularly. Of course, people still clung to the idea of massive resistance the way the Lost Cause continues to speak to people who fly the Confederate flag. But many of those old Confederate symbols are now being removed from the public square, dragged off Monument Avenue in Richmond and installed in nameless warehouses where they will collect dust indefinitely.

And then there's the statue of Harry Byrd that once stood in Capitol Square. Like all the Confederate statues that have been deposed, Harry Byrd recently succumbed to the same fate. In 2021, the baggage of his racist past was just too much to bear. The Democratic majority in the General Assembly passed a bill to remove it and store it away somewhere. Ironically, some Republicans opposed removing the Byrd statue from Capitol Square.

"He was a man of a certain time and a certain era," said Republican Senator Jill Vogel of Fauquier County, who voted against the bill. "So I would just ask the members of this body to look at the whole man and consider that we are each a sum of all our parts."

Lawmakers responded that they had, in fact, looked at the whole man. And they still wanted the statue gone.

"We are still dealing with the aftermath of that with inequity in our schools, inequity in our neighborhoods, inequity in every system we have in Virginia," said Democratic Senator Jennifer McClellan of Richmond. "And because we don't talk about it, we're still trying to figure out how to grapple with it."[204]

More than half a century after his death, the legacy of Harry Byrd is the inequality his machine fought so hard to preserve. Certainly, the union-

Author Michael Lee Pope contemplates the portrait of Harry Byrd outside the Senate chamber in the capitol. *Photo by Craig Carper.*

busting tactics he employed and his pathological hatred of debt are also part of that legacy. But many Virginians—Black and white—will never forgive him for opting to shut down public schools instead of integrating them. He may have wanted to be remembered for opposition to the New Deal and the Great Society, but the enduring monument to his memory is the lost generation of schoolchildren who were denied an education during an unsuccessful fight for white supremacy.

These days, Byrd has two portraits at Virginia's Capitol. One is the young man in a hurry, the portrait of a governor in a dark business suit who has just completed a successful term as governor by implementing a pay-as-you-go philosophy that kept the commonwealth out of debt. The other portrait is the elder statesman, the senior senator from the Old Dominion in a white linen suit trying to preserve a way of life that's perhaps best described as "Gone with the Wind." The first portrait didn't have to become the second. He could have modernized with the times and adapted when necessary. But that didn't happen. Instead, he became a man of a certain time in a certain era—embalmed in that white linen suit and forever in charge of a mythological machine that still haunts Virginia today.

NOTES

Introduction

1. "The Gravest Crisis," *TIME* magazine (September 22, 1958): 16.
2. Cabell Phillips, "New Rumblings in the Old Dominion," *New York Times*, June 19, 1949, Sunday Magazine, 10.
3. J. Harvie Wilkinson III, *Harry Byrd and the Changing Face of Virginia Politics, 1945–1966* (Charlottesville: University Press of Virginia, 1968), 14.
4. Ibid., 22.
5. Ibid.

Chapter 1

6. C. Vann Woodward, *Origins of the New South, 1877–1913: A History of the South* (Baton Rouge: Louisiana State University Press, 1951, reprinted in 1995), 96.
7. Charles Chilton Pearson, *The Readjuster Movement in Virginia* (New Haven, CT: Yale University Press, 1917), 159.
8. *Boston Traveler*, June 19, 1886.
9. Tim McGlone, "What's in a Name: Disputanta," *Virginian Pilot*, April 23, 2013.

10. James T. Moore, "The Death of the Duel: The Code Duello in Readjuster Virginia, 1879–1883," *Virginia Magazine of History and Biography* 83, no. 3 (July 1975): 264.

11. "Speech of Hon. H.H. Riddleberger," *Shenandoah Herald*, March 24, 1880, 1.

12. Virginius Dabney, *Virginia: The New Dominion* (Charlottesville: University Press of Virginia, 1971), 386, 388.

13. "Colonel Cameron Sends to the General Assembly His First Message as Governor," *Richmond Dispatch*, January 7, 1882, 1.

14. Allen Moger, "The Origin of the Democratic Machine in Virginia," *Journal of Southern History* 8 (May 1942): 185.

15. "Coalition Rule in Danville," *Danville Circular*, October 1883, Broadside 1882, Special Collections, Library of Virginia, Richmond, Virginia.

16. "The Riot in Danville," *Staunton Spectator*, November 6, 1883, 2.

17. Charles Noel, "Danville Riot," November 3, 1883, in *Report of Committee of Forty with Sworn Testimony of Thirty-Seven Witnesses &c.* (Richmond, VA: Johns & Goolsby, 1883), 11–13.

18. Brendan Wolfe, "Danville Riot (1883)," *Encyclopedia Virginia*, Virginia Humanities, 2015.

Chapter 2

19. "Gen. Fitzhugh Lee Wins," *New York Times*, July 30, 1885, 5.

20. Allen Moger, *Virginia: Bourbonism to Byrd, 1870–1925* (Charlottesville: University Press of Virginia, 1968), 56.

21. Richard Hamm, "The Killing of John R. Moffett and the Trial of J.T. Clark: Race, Prohibition and Politics in Danville, 1887–1893," *Virginia Magazine of History and Biography* 101, no. 3 (July 1993): 377.

22. "Eighteen Years of Ring Make Change Imperative," *Richmond Times-Dispatch*, August 12, 1911, 1–2.

23. "Proud of It Then, Proud of It Now; Martin's Reply," *Richmond Times-Dispatch*, September 2, 1911, 1.

24. "Thomas S. Martin Is Dead After Long Illness," *Richmond Times-Dispatch*, November 13, 1919, 1.

25. "Swanson and Montague Meet in Exciting Joint Discussion," *Richmond Times*, May 21, 1901, 1.

26. Virginius Dabney, *Virginia: The New Dominion* (Charlottesville: University Press of Virginia, 1971), 430.

27. *Report on the Proceedings and Debates of the Constitutional Convention, State of Virginia*, vol. 2 (Richmond, VA: Heritage Press), 3,076.

28. *Alexandria Gazette*, January 2, 1902, 2.

29. Wuthe Holt, "The Virginia Constitutional Convention of 1901–1902: A Reform Movement Which Lacked Substance," *Virginia Magazine of History and Biography* 68, no. 1 (January 1968).

30. "A Set-to Over Political Affairs," *Richmond Times Dispatch*, August 29, 1905, 3.

31. Ibid.

32. "Changes Stir Up Much Discussion," *Richmond Times-Dispatch*, January 7, 1906, 1.

33. *Accomac Peninsula Enterprise*, August 19, 1905, 4.

34. "Great Campaign Is Past; Day of Balloting Is at Hand," *Richmond Times-Dispatch*, August 22, 1905, 1.

35. "Mr. Martin as Senate Leader," *Washington Post*, November 15, 1916, 6.

36. Jesse Frederick Essary, "A Great Leader Passes," *Richmond Times-Dispatch*, November 13, 1919, 2.

Chapter 3

37. "George P. Coleman's Noblesse Oblige," *Richmond Times-Dispatch*, June 19, 1948, 6.

38. "Coleman Absent From Meeting," *Accomac Peninsula Enterprise*, December 10, 1921, 6.

39. "Trinkle Prejudges the Case," *Richmond Times Dispatch*, May 24, 1921, 4.

40. "E. Lee Trinkle Becomes Governor of Virginia," *Richmond Times-Dispatch*, February 2, 1922, 6.

41. Ibid.

42. Elbert Lee Trinkle to Robert Pennington, February 18, 1922, Trinkle Executive Papers, Library of Virginia.

43. "Trinkle Urges Assembly to Pass Road Bond Issue," *Harrisonburg Daily News Record*, March 4, 1922, 1.

44. "Trinkle and the Bond Issue," *Alexandria Gazette*, February 28, 1922, 2.

45. "Goolrick Assails State Legislature," *Progress and Index Appeal*, March 12, 1922, 11.

46. "Good Roads Assembly Trinkle's Big Chance Is Belief of Goolrick," *Richmond Times Dispatch*, September 10, 1922, 1.

47. "Governor Trinkle's Message to the General Assembly," *Richmond Times-Dispatch*, March 1, 1923, 9.

48. Stanley Willis, "To Lead Virginia Out of the Mud," *Virginia Magazine of History and Biography* 94, no. 4 (October 1986): 448.

49. Ibid., 451.

Chapter 4

50. Aldon Hatch, *The Byrds of Virginia* (New York: Holt, Rinehart and Winston, 1969), 402.

51. Ibid., 406.

52. "Byrd Career Varied and Successful from Boyhood," *Richmond Times Dispatch*, February 1, 1926, 11.

53. Ibid., 11.

54. Hatch, *Byrds of Virginia*, 414.

55. "Another Day and Night of Democratic National Convention Pass and No Choice of Party's Presidential Candidates Has Been Reached," *Richmond Times Dispatch*, June 29, 1912, 1.

56. Hatch, *Byrds of Virginia*, 236.

57. "Would Reorganize State Road Work," *Richmond Times Dispatch*, January 3, 1916, 1.

58. "A Threat to Good Roads," *Richmond Times Dispatch*, January 16, 1916, 16.

59. "Road Builders Adopt Program" *Richmond Times Dispatch*, January 20, 1916, 1.

60. "League to Stand by Convention," *Richmond Times*, January 18, 1902, 2.

61. "Norfolk View of Our Politics," *Richmond Times Dispatch*, March 17, 1909, 6.

62. Hatch, *Byrds of Virginia*, 419.

63. "Byrd Denounces Latest Attacks of His Foes as False, Vile, Malicious," *Richmond Times-Dispatch*, July 10, 1925, 1.

64. "Mapp Says Byrd Misrepresents His Tax Equalization Program," *Richmond Times-Dispatch*, July 25, 1925, 1.

65. "Byrd Easy Winner," *Richmond Times-Dispatch*, August 5, 1925, 1.

Chapter 5

66. Marshall Fishwick, *Virginia: A New Look at the Old Dominion* (New York: Harper and Brothers, 1959).

67. "Mrs. Trinkle and Son, Lee, Narrowly Escape with their Lives as Flames Sweep Mansion," *Richmond Times-Dispatch*, January 5, 1926.

68. "Large Crowd Is Present at Governor's Reception," *Richmond Times-Dispatch*, February 2, 1926, 8.

69. Hatch, *Byrds of Virginia*, 425.

70. Ibid., 425.

71. Ibid., 426.

72. Ibid., 428.

73. "Byrd Urges Reduction in Number of State Departments," *Richmond Times-Dispatch*, February 4, 1926, 7.

74. "Convention Keynote Orator Sees Dawn of New Day in Politics in Old Dominion," *Richmond Times-Dispatch*, June 27, 1929, 8.

75. "Short Ballot Wins in Senate, 27 to 12, After Hot Debate," *Richmond Times-Dispatch*, February 3, 1928, 1.

76. Ibid.

77. "Virginia Not So Slow," *Richmond Times-Dispatch* editorial, February 22, 1926, 12.

78. "Governor Sees Election Mandate for Efficiency," *Richmond Times-Dispatch*, February 2, 1926, 7.

79. Louis Jaffé to Harry Byrd, January 12, 1929, Harry Byrd Executive Papers, Library of Virginia.

80. Virginius Dabney, *Richmond: The Story of a City* (Charlottesville: University Press of Virginia, 1976), 317.

81. Hatch, *Byrds of Virginia*, 430.

82. Virginia Lee Cox, "Ocean Flight Failures Little Affect Commercial Aviation, Lindy Avers," *Richmond Times-Dispatch*, October 16, 1927.

83. Hatch, *Byrds of Virginia*, 431.

84. "Republicans Pile Up Leave of 20,000 with 1,414 Precincts Given," *Richmond Times-Dispatch*, November 7, 1928, 1.

85. Hatch, *Byrds of Virginia*, 433.

86. "Pollard Will Be Contender in Race for Governorship," *Richmond Times-Dispatch*, March 3, 1929, 1.

87. "Pollard Leads Ticket to Overwhelming Victory," *Richmond Times-Dispatch*, November 6, 1929, 1.

Chapter 6

88. Brent Tarter, "A Flier on the National Scene: Harry F. Byrd's Favorite-Son Presidential Candidacy of 1932," *Virginia Magazine of History and Biography* 82, no. 3 (July 1974): 304–5.

89. "Byrd Indorsed for President by Assembly," *Richmond Times-Dispatch*, January 15, 1932, 7.

90. Virginius Dabney, "Aid for Byrd Is Seen in Smith Statement," *New York Times*, February 14, 1932, 70.

91. Tarter, "Flier on the National Scene," 289.

92. Ibid., 293.

93. Ibid., 295.

94. "Prohibition, Tariff, Government Economy Points in Byrd's Speech," *Richmond Times-Dispatch*, June 10, 1932, 8.

95. "Rogers Chats with Candidates; Finds Byrd 'High-Class Man,'" *Richmond Times-Dispatch*, June 27, 1932, 5.

96. "Glass Names Ex-Governor; Breckinridge Seconds Him," *Richmond Times-Dispatch*, July 1, 1932, 1.

97. Ibid., 8.

98. James Farley, *Behind the Ballots* (New York: Harcourt, Brace, 1939), 137–38.

99. "Byrd Releases Vote, Delegates Go to Roosevelt," *Richmond Times-Dispatch*, July 2, 1932, 4.

100. Tarter, "Flier on the National Scene," 305.

Chapter 7

101. J. Harvie Wilkinson, *Harry Byrd and the Changing Face of Virginia Politics* (Charlottesville: University Press of Virginia, 1968), 27.

102. Charles Houston, *Virginians in Congress* (Richmond, VA: Richmond Newspapers, 1966), 13.

103. Wilkinson, *Harry Byrd*, 25.

104. W.B. Crawley Jr., "William M. Tuck (1896–1983)," *Encyclopedia Virginia*, July 12, 2018.

105. Ibid.

106. "Tuck Opposes Government Employee Unionization," *Richmond Times-Dispatch*, January 22, 1946, 1.

107. Hartsfield to Tuck, January 31. 1946, Tuck Executive Papers.

108. "Pugh Scores 'Anti-Labor' Tuck Message," *Richmond Times-Dispatch*, January 22, 1946, 1.

109. "Time Presses Passage of Primary Bill," *Bluefield Daily Telegraph*, January 24, 1946, 1.

110. "Byrd Proposes Unions File with SEC," *Richmond Times Dispatch*, January 24, 1946, 1.

111. "Two Strikes May Disrupt Utilities in State," *Richmond Times-Dispatch*, January 13, 1946.

112. William Crawley, *Bill Tuck: A Political Life in Harry Byrd's Virginia* (Charlottesville: University Press of Virginia, 1978), 94.

113. "State Seizure Promised if Vepco Workers Strike," *Richmond Times-Dispatch*, March 23, 1946, 1.

114. "Strike at Vepco Is Imminent as Wage Talks Fail," *Richmond Times-Dispatch*, March 27, 1946, 1.

115. "Militia Mobilized as Tuck Acts in Vepco Dispute," *Richmond Times-Dispatch*, March 29, 1946.

116. Marvin Schlegel, *Virginia on Guard: Civilian Defense and the State Militia in the Second World War* (Richmond: Virginia State Library, 1949), 247–48.

117. "Militia Moves Swiftly to Induct Vepco Workers," *Richmond Times-Dispatch*, March 30, 1946, 1.

118. "Vepco Workers Accept Orders to Go on Duty with Militia as Jokes Cover Displeasure," *Richmond Times-Dispatch*, March 30, 1946, 4.

119. Ibid.

120. "Tuck, Byrd Denounced by Union Men," *Richmond Times-Dispatch*, March 30, 1946, 1.

121. "Norfolk Group Wires Protest to Governor," *Richmond Times-Dispatch*, March 30, 1946, 4.

122. "Tuck's Forceful Action," *Danville Bee*, March 30, 1946, 6.

123. Benjamin Mears to Tuck, August 8, 1946, Tuck Executive Papers, Library of Virginia.

124. Bill Tuck to Harry Byrd, April 2, 1946, Byrd Executive Papers, Library of Virginia.

125. *Congressional Record*, May 27, 1946, 5,791.

126. "Text of Governor's Message on Labor Measures, Schools to Special Assembly Session," *Richmond Times-Dispatch*, January 7, 1947, 4.

127. "Union Spokesmen Turn Heaviest Guns on Tuck's Proposed Labor Legislation at Joint Senate, House Public Hearing," *Richmond Times Dispatch*, January 10, 1947, 1.

128. Ibid.

129. Ibid.

130. "Lesson for Labor Leaders," *Richmond Times-Dispatch*, January 12, 1947, 2D.

131. "Governor's Labor Legislation Appears Assured of Gaining Passage in House," *Richmond Times-Dispatch*, January 14, 1947, 1.

132. Ibid.

133. "Tuck's Labor Bills Pass," *Richmond Times-Dispatch*, January 17, 1947, 1.

134. Crawley, *Bill Tuck*, 121–22.

135. Ibid., 133.

Chapter 8

136. James Latimer, "Assembly Fights May Boomerang on Organization," *Richmond Times-Dispatch*, March 19, 1950, 1B.

137. Homer Richey, "Says Boothe Proposal Won't Satisfy Demand for Equality," *Richmond Times-Dispatch*, January 15, 1950, 2D.

138. "Darden Backs Bill to Modify Segregation," *Richmond Times-Dispatch*, February 23, 1950, A1.

139. Parke Rouse, "Antisegregation Bill Killed; Legislators Say Folks at Home Opposed," *Richmond Times-Dispatch*, February 26, 1950, D1.

140. Peter Henriques, "The Byrd Organization Crushes a Liberal Challenge, 1950–1953," *Virginia Magazine of History and Biography* 87, no. 1 (January 1979): 5.

141. Guy Friddel, *What Is It About Virginia?* (Richmond, VA: Dietz Press, 1966), 70.

142. Henriques, "Byrd Organization Crushes a Liberal Challenge," 8.

143. James Latimer, "Teacher Pay Hike Killed, Assembly Ends," *Richmond Times-Dispatch*, March 13, 1950, A1.

144. "Chance for Senate Committee to do a Service on Poll Tax," *Richmond Times-Dispatch*, February 26, 1952, A12.

145. Charles McDowell, "Capitol Sidelights," *Richmond Times-Dispatch*, March 7, 1954, B1.

146. James Latimer, "House Votes to Use Byrd Tax Money," *Richmond Times-Dispatch*, March 4, 1954, A1.

147. Ibid.

148. James Latimer, "Old-Line Chiefs Lost Their Grip on House," *Richmond Times-Dispatch*, March 16, 1954, A1.

149. Ibid.

150. Douglas Smith, "When Reason Collides with Prejudice: Armistead Boothe and the Politics of Desegregation in Virginia, 1948–1963," *Virginia Magazine of History and Biography* 102, no. 1 (January 1994): 19.

151. Benjamin Muse, "Young Turks Slightly Left of Sultan," *Washington Post*, March 28, 1954, B2.

Chapter 9

152. "Farmville Citizens Canvassed on Public School Segregation," *Winchester Evening Star*, April 27, 1951, 11.

153. "Long Strike Is Forecast," *Pulaski Southwest Times*, April 29, 1951, 2.

154. "Educational Segregation Suit Opens," *Richmond Times-Dispatch*, February 26, 1952, 1.

155. "School Segregation Is Upheld," *Richmond Times-Dispatch*, March 8, 1952, 1.

156. Hatch, *Byrds of Virginia*, 497.

157. Ibid.

158. "Poff Sees Court 'Cutting Puppy's Tail' Little at a Time So It Won't Hurt Much," *Richmond Times-Dispatch*, June 2, 1955, 5.

159. James Latimer, "Stanley to Confer on State's Next Step," *Richmond Times-Dispatch*, May 18, 1954, 1.

160. "Court to Reopen Segregation Debate," *Richmond Times-Dispatch*, September 23, 1954, 1.

161. James Latimer, "32 Assembly Members Appointed to Chart Course on Segregation Issue," *Richmond Times-Dispatch*, August 29, 1954, 1.

162. "Three Segregation Views Emerge at Herring Here," *Richmond Times-Dispatch*, November 16, 1954, 1.

163. Ibid.

164. "The Gray Commission's Good Report," *Richmond Times-Dispatch*, November 13, 1955, 2D.

165. "Gray Report Looks Good to Many in Assembly," *Richmond Times-Dispatch*, November 14, 1955, 1.

166. Charles McDowell, "Senator Byrd Speaks Out on Behalf of Referendum," *Richmond Times-Dispatch*, December 18, 1955, 1.

167. "Forum Speakers View Situation if Gray Plan Wins," *Richmond Times-Dispatch*, January 6, 1956, 5.

168. "General Assembly Votes Interposition Resolution," *Richmond Times-Dispatch*, February 2, 1956, 1.

169. Ibid.

170. "Sen. Byrd Urges Southern States to Stand Together," *Winchester Evening Star*, February 27, 1956, 2.

171. Dabney, *Virginia*, 537.

172. James Latimer, "Anti-Integration Course Is Charted by Assembly," *Richmond Times-Dispatch*, September 22, 1956, 1.

173. "Dalton 'Surrender' Assailed by Almond," *Richmond Times-Dispatch*, October 10, 1957, 4.

174. "Gravest Crisis," 16.

175. "Sen. Byrd Expresses Appreciation," *Winchester Evening Star*, November 5, 1958, 1.

176. Roger Greene, "Almond Faces School Crisis," *Richmond Times-Dispatch*, September 21, 1958, 21.

177. "Willey Suggests School Study Now," *Richmond Times-Dispatch*, November 20, 1958, 1.

178. "What Will Happen Next Is Va. School Problem," *Radford News Journal*, January 20, 1959, 1.

179. "Text of Governor's Address on Schools," *Richmond Times-Dispatch*, January 21, 1959, 4.

180. "Text of Governor's Address," January 29, 1959, 1.

181. Dabney, *Virginia*, 543.

182. "Desegregation Normal," *Washington Post*, February 3, 1959, A16.

183. Allan Jones, "Senate, by 30-to-6 Vote, Approves Perrow Compulsory Attendance Bill," *Richmond Times-Dispatch*, April 23, 1959, A6.

184. Wilkinson, *Harry Byrd*, 113.

185. Carl Shires, "Sen. Harry Byrd Never Spoke to Gov. Almond in 7 Years," *Martinsville Bulletin*, October 6, 1967, A1.

Chapter 10

186. James Latimer, "Is Byrd Machine Being Retooled?," *Richmond Times-Dispatch*, January 3, 1965, 1.

187. Frank B. Atkinson, *The Dynamic Dominion* (Lanham, MD: Rowman & Littlefield Publishers, 2006), 161.

188. James Latimer, "Godwin Enters Race for Virginia Governor," *Richmond Times-Dispatch*, January 10, 1965, 1.

189. William Chapman, "Mills Godwin Is Man to Catch as Virginia's Governor Race Begins," *Washington Post*, November 12, 1964, D22.

190. Lynwood Holton, *Opportunity Time* (Charlottesville: University of Virginia Press, 2008), 57.

191. "Conservatives Nominate Ticket Headed by Story," *Richmond Times-Dispatch*, July 11, 1965, 1.

192. "U.S. Nazi Chief to Be Candidate for Governor," *Richmond Times-Dispatch*, April 20, 1965, 3.

193. James Sweeney, "Bridge to the New Dominion," *Virginia Magazine of History and Biography* 125, no. 3 (2017): 260.

194. Helen Dewar, "Sen. Byrd Rallies Conservatives to Godwin Ticket," *Washington Post*, October 21, 1965, B1.

195. Helen Dewar, "AFL-CIO Endorses Godwin's Candidacy," *Washington Post*, October 13, 1965, A1.

196. Helen Dewar, "Virginia Democrats Eye Negro Vote," *Washington Post*, October 15, 1965, B1.

197. Helen Dewar, "Klan's Virginia Drive Considered a Minor Irritant," *Washington Post*, September 21, 1965, A4.

198. Allen Jones, "State Conservatives Rap Godwin, Holton," *Richmond Times-Dispatch*, August 20, 1965, A1.

199. "Rockwell Shows Rifle in Speech," *Richmond Times-Dispatch*, September 12, 1965, 4B.

200. Helen Dewar, "Personalities Clash in Va. Campaign," *Washington Post*, October 12, 1965, c1.

201. "Our Choice for Election," *Richmond Times-Dispatch*, October 24, 1965, B14.

202. "A Night of Surprises," *Richmond News Leader*, November 3, 1965, 6.

Epilogue

203. James Latimer, "Holton Defeated Battle for Governor, Becomes 1st GOP Winner of Century," *Richmond Times Dispatch*, November 5, 1969, A1.

204. Michael Pope, "Virginia Senate Votes to Remove Harry Byrd Statue from Capitol Square," WVTF, February 23, 2021.

INDEX

ABOUT THE AUTHOR

Michael Lee Pope is an award-winning journalist and podcaster who lives in Old Town Alexandria. He has reported for NPR, the *New York Times* and *Northern Virginia Magazine*. He has a master's degree in American studies from Florida State University, and he is a former adjunct professor at Tallahassee Community College.

Visit us at
www.historypress.com